Grade 1

Treasures

SO-BMR-981

Teacher's Resource Book

Mc Graw Hill Macmillan McGraw-Hill

Photography Credits

238: Comstock. 240: C Squared Studios/Getty Images.

The McGraw·Hill Companies

Mc **Macmillan**
Graw **McGraw-Hill**
Hill

Published by Macmillan/McGraw-Hill, of McGraw-Hill Education, a division of The McGraw-Hill Companies, Inc., Two Penn Plaza, New York, New York 10121.

Printed in the United States of America

5 6 7 8 9 10 024 11 10 09 08 07

Contents

Weekly Student Contracts..**2**

Using the *Weekly Student Contracts* 2

Foldables™ by Dinah Zike.................................**33**

Welcome and General Information 33

Directions and Applications 37

Foldables Correlated to Reading Skills 64

Word Study...**65**

Picture Cards 66

Alphabet Letter Cards 88

Spelling Word Cards 90

Vocabulary Word Cards 120

Sound Boxes 150

Games 152

Additional Literacy Support.........................**165**

Rhymes and Chimes 166

Story Patterns 196

Reader Response Sheets 227

Writer's Checklists 230

Proofreading Marks...232

Writing Rubric 233

Picture Prompts 234

Award Certificate 241

Handwriting 242

Classroom Behavior Checklist 254

Weekly Student Contracts

Helping Children Manage Their Time

Weekly Student Contracts help children manage their independent work time.

A Student Contract is supplied for each week of instruction in Treasures. The contract lists independent activities provided in the program that support priority skills for the week. The activities listed include:

- workstation activities
- leveled readers and activities
- technology activities
- practice book activities

Name _____ Date _____

My To-Do List

✔ Put a check next to the activities you complete.

Reading
- ☐ Read a book
- ☐ Reread the story

Word Work
- ☐ Build short *a* words
- ☐ Sort words

Writing
- ☐ Draw yourself
- ☐ Draw what you like to do

Science
- ☐ Draw your face
- ☐ Draw food

Social Studies
- ☐ Draw your home
- ☐ Write about home

Leveled Readers
- ☐ Write About It!
- ☐ Content Connection

Technology
- ☐ Buggles and Beezy
- ☐ Vocabulary Puzzlemaker
- ☐ Fluency Solutions
- ☐ Listening Library

Independent Practice
- ☐ Practice Book, 1–8
- ☐ Grammar Book, 1–5
- ☐ Spelling Book, 1–4

Contracts   Unit 1 • Pam and Sam ③

© Macmillan/McGraw-Hill

How to Use the Student Contract

- At the beginning of each week, distribute a contract to each child.

- Discuss with children each activity listed in the contract.

- Identify activities and practice book pages that you expect children to complete by the end of the week.

- As children complete each assigned activity, ask them to check off the completed task on the contract and store their work in a folder.

- Children can choose other activities from the contract after completing the assigned activities.

- Check the work in the folder at the end of each week. The folder can also be sent home for review.

My To-Do List

✔ Put a check next to the activities you complete.

📖 Reading

- ☐ Read a book
- ☐ Reread the story

🔤 Word Work

- ☐ Build short *a* words
- ☐ Sort words

✏️ Writing

- ☐ Draw yourself
- ☐ Draw what you like to do

🔍 Science

- ☐ Draw your face
- ☐ Draw food

🌎 Social Studies

- ☐ Draw your home
- ☐ Write about home

📖 Leveled Readers

- ☐ Write About It!
- ☐ Content Connection

🖱️ Technology

- ☐ Buggles and Beezy
- ☐ Vocabulary Puzzlemaker
- ☐ Fluency Solutions
- ☐ Listening Library

🖌️ Independent Practice

- ☐ Practice Book, 1–8
- ☐ Grammar Book, 1–5
- ☐ Spelling Book, 1–4

My To-Do List

✔ Put a check next to the activities you complete.

📖 Reading

- ☐ Read a book
- ☐ Read to a partner

🄰🄱🄲 Word Work

- ☐ Build short *a* words
- ☐ Sort words

✏️ Writing

- ☐ Write about sports
- ☐ Write about playgrounds

🔍 Science

- ☐ Make an animal mask
- ☐ Draw an animal

🌎 Social Studies

- ☐ List ways to get around
- ☐ Draw a favorite way

📖 Leveled Readers

- ☐ Write About It!
- ☐ Content Connection

🖱️ Technology

- ☐ Buggles and Beezy
- ☐ Vocabulary Puzzlemaker
- ☐ Fluency Solutions
- ☐ Listening Library

✏️ Independent Practice

- ☐ Practice Book, 9-16
- ☐ Grammar Book, 6-10
- ☐ Spelling Book, 5-8

Contracts

My To-Do List

✔ Put a check next to the activities you complete.

Reading

☐ Read a book
☐ Read with a partner

Word Work

☐ Draw and label words
☐ Sort words

Writing

☐ Write about learning
☐ Write about food

Science

☐ Draw three animals
☐ Label the animals

Social Studies

☐ Write about growing up
☐ Talk about getting big

Leveled Readers

☐ Write About It!
☐ Content Connection

Technology

☐ Buggles and Beezy
☐ Vocabulary Puzzlemaker
☐ Fluency Solutions
☐ Listening Library

Independent Practice

☐ Practice Book, 17–24
☐ Grammar Book, 11–15
☐ Spelling Book, 9–12

© Macmillan/McGraw-Hill

My To-Do List

✔ Put a check next to the activities you complete.

📖 Reading

- ☐ Read with a partner
- ☐ Reread the story

🔤 Word Work

- ☐ Build *r* blend words
- ☐ Search for *r* blend words

✏️ Writing

- ☐ Write about pet homes
- ☐ Count pets

🔍 Science

- ☐ Write what pets need
- ☐ Make a pet care book

🌎 Social Studies

- ☐ Learn about vets
- ☐ Draw people helping

📖 Leveled Readers

- ☐ Write About It!
- ☐ Content Connection

🖱️ Technology

- ☐ Buggles and Beezy
- ☐ Vocabulary Puzzlemaker
- ☐ Fluency Solutions
- ☐ Listening Library

📝 Independent Practice

- ☐ Practice Book, 25–32
- ☐ Grammar Book, 16–20
- ☐ Spelling Book, 13–16

Name _____ Date _____

My To-Do List

✔ Put a check next to the activities you complete.

Reading
- [ ] Read a book
- [ ] Retell the story

Word Work
- [ ] Build end blend words
- [ ] Write *-st* words

Writing
- [ ] Write about a team
- [ ] Make a teamwork collage

Science
- [ ] Think about ways to keep school clean
- [ ] Make a list of ways

Social Studies
- [ ] Talk about teamwork
- [ ] Write about team sports

Leveled Readers
- [ ] Write About It!
- [ ] Content Connection

Technology
- [ ] Buggles and Beezy
- [ ] Vocabulary Puzzlemaker
- [ ] Fluency Solutions
- [ ] Listening Library

Independent Practice
- [ ] Practice Book, 33–40
- [ ] Grammar Book, 21–25
- [ ] Spelling Book, 17–20

My To-Do List

✔ **Put a check next to the activities you complete.**

📖 Reading

- ☐ Pick a book to read
- ☐ Read to a partner

🔤 Word Work

- ☐ Sort short *o* words
- ☐ Write short *o* words

✏️ Writing

- ☐ Draw and label an animal family
- ☐ Write about animals

🔍 Science

- ☐ Draw an animal and her baby
- ☐ List their differences

🌎 Social Studies

- ☐ Draw an animal family
- ☐ Write about their home

📖 Leveled Readers

- ☐ Write About It!
- ☐ Content Connection

🖱️ Technology

- ☐ Buggles and Beezy
- ☐ Vocabulary Puzzlemaker
- ☐ Fluency Solutions
- ☐ Listening Library

📝 Independent Practice

- ☐ Practice Book, 43-50
- ☐ Grammar Book, 26-30
- ☐ Spelling Book, 21-24

Name _____ Date _____

My To-Do List

✔ **Put a check next to the activities you complete.**

📖 Reading

- ☐ Pick a story to read
- ☐ Retell the story

Word Work

- ☐ Build short *e* words
- ☐ Sort short *e* rhyming words

Writing

- ☐ Draw and label a job
- ☐ Draw and label a sandwich

Science

- ☐ Draw yourself helping
- ☐ Tell how you help

Social Studies

- ☐ Draw a person's job
- ☐ Draw a job you'd like

Leveled Readers

- ☐ Write About It!
- ☐ Content Connection

Technology

- ☐ Buggles and Beezy
- ☐ Vocabulary Puzzlemaker
- ☐ Fluency Solutions
- ☐ Listening Library

Independent Practice

- ☐ Practice Book, 51–58
- ☐ Grammar Book, 31–35
- ☐ Spelling Book, 25–28

My To-Do List

✔ Put a check next to the activities you complete.

📕 Reading

- ☐ Read a book
- ☐ Read for main idea

🔤 Word Work

- ☐ Build words with *th*, *sh*
- ☐ Sort words with *th*, *sh*

✏️ Writing

- ☐ Draw an animal's home
- ☐ Write about it

🔍 Science

- ☐ Tell where animals live
- ☐ Write about them

🌎 Social Studies

- ☐ Talk about animals in different places
- ☐ Write about them

📖 Leveled Readers

- ☐ Write About It!
- ☐ Content Connection

🖱️ Technology

- ☐ Buggles and Beezy
- ☐ Vocabulary Puzzlemaker
- ☐ Fluency Solutions
- ☐ Listening Library

✍️ Independent Practice

- ☐ Practice Book, 59–66
- ☐ Grammar Book, 36–40
- ☐ Spelling Book, 29–32

My To-Do List

✔ Put a check next to the activities you complete.

📖 Reading

- [ ] Pick a book to read
- [ ] Use Retelling Cards

🔤 Word Work

- [ ] Write short *u* words
- [ ] Sort short *u* words

✏️ Writing

- [ ] Label an instrument
- [ ] Write about an animal band

🔍 Science

- [ ] Draw something you hear
- [ ] Write about the sound

🌎 Social Studies

- [ ] Draw a parade
- [ ] Write about a parade

📖 Leveled Readers

- [ ] Write About It!
- [ ] Content Connection

🖱️ Technology

- [ ] Buggles and Beezy
- [ ] Vocabulary Puzzlemaker
- [ ] Fluency Solutions
- [ ] Listening Library

✍️ Independent Practice

- [ ] Practice Book, 67–74
- [ ] Grammar Book, 41–45
- [ ] Spelling Book, 33–36

My To-Do List

✔ Put a check next to the activities you complete.

📖 Reading

- [ ] Pick a book to read
- [ ] Read with a partner

(ABC) Word Work

- [ ] Build / blend words
- [ ] Sort / blend words

✏️ Writing

- [ ] Draw and label a picture
- [ ] Write about a shape

🔍 Science

- [ ] Draw the weather
- [ ] Write about weather

🌎 Social Studies

- [ ] Draw children in another country
- [ ] Write about their day

📖 Leveled Readers

- [ ] Write About It!
- [ ] Content Connection

🖱️ Technology

- [ ] Buggles and Beezy
- [ ] Vocabulary Puzzlemaker
- [ ] Fluency Solutions
- [ ] Listening Library

✏️ Independent Practice

- [ ] Practice Book, 75–82
- [ ] Grammar Book, 46–50
- [ ] Spelling Book, 37–40

Contracts

Name _____ Date _____

My To-Do List

✔ Put a check next to the activities you complete.

📖 Reading
- ☐ Read a book
- ☐ Read with a partner

Ⓐ Word Work
- ☐ Build long *a* words
- ☐ Sort words

✏️ Writing
- ☐ Write to a friend
- ☐ Draw friends

🔍 Science
- ☐ Measure steps
- ☐ Write about steps

🌎 Social Studies
- ☐ Draw a map
- ☐ Write directions

📖 Leveled Readers
- ☐ Write About It!
- ☐ Content Connection

🖱️ Technology
- ☐ Buggles and Beezy
- ☐ Vocabulary Puzzlemaker
- ☐ Fluency Solutions
- ☐ Listening Library

Independent Practice
- ☐ Practice Book, 85–92
- ☐ Grammar Book, 51–55
- ☐ Spelling Book, 41–44

© Macmillan/McGraw-Hill

My To-Do List

✔ Put a check next to the activities you complete.

📖 Reading

- ☐ Read a book
- ☐ Read with a partner

🅰️🅱️🅲️ Word Work

- ☐ Build *s* blend words
- ☐ Sort words

✏️ Writing

- ☐ Write about helping
- ☐ Draw a picture

🔍 Science

- ☐ Draw and label things
- ☐ Write about a drawing

🌎 Social Studies

- ☐ Draw kids of the world
- ☐ Use a map

📖 Leveled Readers

- ☐ Write About It!
- ☐ Content Connection

🖱️ Technology

- ☐ Buggles and Beezy
- ☐ Vocabulary Puzzlemaker
- ☐ Fluency Solutions
- ☐ Listening Library

🖌️ Independent Practice

- ☐ Practice Book, 93–100
- ☐ Grammar Book, 56–60
- ☐ Spelling Book, 45–48

My To-Do List

✔ **Put a check next to the activities you complete.**

 ## Reading

☐ Read a book
☐ Read with a partner

Ⓐ Ⓑ Ⓒ Word Work

☐ Build words with *ch*, *wh*, *tch*
☐ Sort words

 ## Writing

☐ Write about shadows
☐ Make animal shadows

Science

☐ Draw a sun picture
☐ Write about the sun

Social Studies

☐ Draw Earth and sun
☐ Write about day and night

Leveled Readers

☐ Write About It!
☐ Content Connection

 ## Technology

☐ Buggles and Beezy
☐ Vocabulary Puzzlemaker
☐ Fluency Solutions
☐ Listening Library

 ## Independent Practice

☐ Practice Book, 101–108
☐ Grammar Book, 61–65
☐ Spelling Book, 49–52

My To-Do List

✔ Put a check next to the activities you complete.

📖 Reading

☐ Read with a partner
☐ Read aloud

🔤 Word Work

☐ Build long *i* words
☐ Sort rhyming words

✏️ Writing

☐ Write about your family
☐ Make family puppets

🔍 Science

☐ Write about summer
☐ Write about winter

🌎 Social Studies

☐ Draw a job
☐ Write about a job

📖 Leveled Readers

☐ Write About It!
☐ Content Connection

🖱️ Technology

☐ Buggles and Beezy
☐ Vocabulary Puzzlemaker
☐ Fluency Solutions
☐ Listening Library

📝 Independent Practice

☐ Practice Book, 109–116
☐ Grammar Book, 66–70
☐ Spelling Book, 53–56

My To-Do List

✔ Put a check next to the activities you complete.

 Reading

☐ Read a book
☐ Read with a partner

 **Word Work**

☐ Build words with *str-, spl-, scr-*
☐ Sort spelling words

 Writing

☐ Write a story
☐ Draw your family

 Science

☐ Draw an animal
☐ Draw an animal family

 Social Studies

☐ Write about celebrating
☐ Draw a celebration

 Leveled Readers

☐ Write About It!
☐ Content Connection

Technology

☐ Buggles and Beezy
☐ Vocabulary Puzzlemaker
☐ Fluency Solutions
☐ Listening Library

 Independent Practice

☐ Practice Book, 117–124
☐ Grammar Book, 71–75
☐ Spelling Book, 57–60

My To-Do List

✔ Put a check next to the activities you complete.

 Reading

☐ Read with a partner
☐ Retell the story

 Word Work

☐ Use a dictionary
☐ Sort spelling words

 Writing

☐ Draw and write about birds
☐ Create bird shapes

 Science

☐ Draw a bird's nest
☐ Learn how nests are made

 Social Studies

☐ Draw where birds live
☐ List local bird types

 Leveled Readers

☐ Write About It!
☐ Content Connection

 Technology

☐ Buggles and Beezy
☐ Vocabulary Puzzlemaker
☐ Fluency Solutions
☐ Listening Library

Independent Practice

☐ Practice Book, 127–135
☐ Grammar Book, 76–80
☐ Spelling Book, 61–64

My To-Do List

✔ **Put a check next to the activities you complete.**

📕 Reading

- ☐ Retell the story
- ☐ Read a book

Ⓐ🄱🄲 Word Work

- ☐ Build long *u* words
- ☐ Play a concentration word game

✏️ Writing

- ☐ Make a poster
- ☐ List old things

🔍 Science

- ☐ List recyclable things
- ☐ Write how recycling helps people

🌎 Social Studies

- ☐ Draw garbage collectors
- ☐ Write about them

📖 Leveled Readers

- ☐ Write About It!
- ☐ Content Connection

🖱️ Technology

- ☐ Buggles and Beezy
- ☐ Vocabulary Puzzlemaker
- ☐ Fluency Solutions
- ☐ Listening Library

📝 Independent Practice

- ☐ Practice Book, 136–144
- ☐ Grammar Book, 81–85
- ☐ Spelling Book, 65–68

My To-Do List

✔ Put a check next to the activities you complete.

Reading

☐ Pick a book
☐ Read on the computer

Word Work

☐ Build words with *ay*, *ai*
☐ Sort spelling word cards

Writing

☐ Write a weather report
☐ Write a new song verse

Science

☐ Use a thermometer
☐ Compare temperatures

Social Studies

☐ Create accordion books
☐ Draw pictures

Leveled Readers

☐ Write About It!
☐ Content Connection

Technology

☐ Buggles and Beezy
☐ Vocabulary Puzzlemaker
☐ Fluency Solutions
☐ Listening Library

Independent Practice

☐ Practice Book, 145–153
☐ Grammar Book, 86–90
☐ Spelling Book, 69–72

Name _____ Date _____

My To-Do List

✔ Put a check next to the activities you complete.

Reading

- [ ] Read with a partner
- [ ] Retell the story

Word Work

- [ ] Build words with *e, ee, ea*
- [ ] Sort words

Writing

- [ ] Write a report
- [ ] Solve problems

Science

- [ ] Use a magnifying glass
- [ ] Figure out a picture

Social Studies

- [ ] Draw a time long ago
- [ ] List and draw inventions

Leveled Readers

- [ ] Write About It!
- [ ] Content Connection

Technology

- [ ] Buggles and Beezy
- [ ] Vocabulary Puzzlemaker
- [ ] Fluency Solutions
- [ ] Listening Library

Independent Practice

- [ ] Practice Book, 154–162
- [ ] Grammar Book, 91–95
- [ ] Spelling Book, 73–76

Name _____ Date _____

My To-Do List

✔ Put a check next to the activities you complete.

📕 Reading

☐ Pick a book
☐ Retell the story

🔤 Word Work

☐ Build long *e* words
☐ Search for words

✏️ Writing

☐ Write a new ending
☐ Put on a puppet show

🔍 Science

☐ Draw an animal
☐ Write how it stays safe

🌎 Social Studies

☐ Draw animal friends
☐ Make a collage

📖 Leveled Readers

☐ Write About It!
☐ Content Connection

🖱️ Technology

☐ Buggles and Beezy
☐ Vocabulary Puzzlemaker
☐ Fluency Solutions
☐ Listening Library

📝 Independent Practice

☐ Practice Book, 163–171
☐ Grammar Book, 96–100
☐ Spelling Book, 77–80

My To-Do List

✔ Put a check next to the activities you complete.

📖 Reading

- ☐ Pick a book
- ☐ Retell the story

Ⓐ🅑🅒 Word Work

- ☐ Build long o words
- ☐ Sort spelling words by patterns

✏️ Writing

- ☐ Write an invitation
- ☐ Write about exercise

🔍 Science

- ☐ Draw and label a cat
- ☐ Draw another animal

🌎 Social Studies

- ☐ Write about an artist
- ☐ Draw a museum

📖 Leveled Readers

- ☐ Write About It!
- ☐ Content Connection

🖱️ Technology

- ☐ Buggles and Beezy
- ☐ Vocabulary Puzzlemaker
- ☐ Fluency Solutions
- ☐ Listening Library

📝 Independent Practice

- ☐ Practice Book, 174–182
- ☐ Grammar Book, 101–105
- ☐ Spelling Book, 81–84

My To-Do List

✔ Put a check next to the activities you complete.

📖 Reading

- [ ] Read with a partner
- [ ] Reread the story

ⒶⒷⒸ Word Work

- [ ] Build long *i* words
- [ ] Sort spelling words by pattern

✏️ Writing

- [ ] Write and draw a story
- [ ] Write about how objects move

🔍 Science

- [ ] Use a magnet
- [ ] Write about things the magnet moves

🌎 Social Studies

- [ ] Draw a street sign
- [ ] Write about signs

📖 Leveled Readers

- [ ] Write About It!
- [ ] Content Connection

🖱️ Technology

- [ ] Buggles and Beezy
- [ ] Vocabulary Puzzlemaker
- [ ] Fluency Solutions
- [ ] Listening Library

🖌️ Independent Practice

- [ ] Practice Book, 183–191
- [ ] Grammar Book, 106–110
- [ ] Spelling Book, 85–88

My To-Do List

✔ Put a check next to the activities you complete.

📕 Reading
- ☐ Pick a book
- ☐ Read a story

ⒶⒷⒸ Word Work
- ☐ Build *ar* words
- ☐ Sort words by ending sounds

✏️ Writing
- ☐ Write about inventions
- ☐ Draw and label pictures

🔍 Science
- ☐ Draw an invention
- ☐ Write about inventions

🌎 Social Studies
- ☐ Talk about telephones
- ☐ Role-play an emergency

📖 Leveled Readers
- ☐ Write About It!
- ☐ Content Connection

🖱️ Technology
- ☐ Buggles and Beezy
- ☐ Vocabulary Puzzlemaker
- ☐ Fluency Solutions
- ☐ Listening Library

Independent Practice
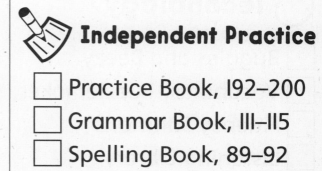
- ☐ Practice Book, 192–200
- ☐ Grammar Book, 111–115
- ☐ Spelling Book, 89–92

My To-Do List

✔ **Put a check next to the activities you complete.**

 Reading

- [ ] Read with a partner
- [ ] Retell the story

 Word Work

- [ ] Build *or* words
- [ ] Sort spelling words

 Writing

- [ ] Write about learning
- [ ] Write about sports

 Science

- [ ] Draw and write about baby animals
- [ ] Learn more about them

 Social Studies

- [ ] Draw a teacher
- [ ] Write about teaching

 Leveled Readers

- [ ] Write About It!
- [ ] Content Connection

Technology

- [ ] Buggles and Beezy
- [ ] Vocabulary Puzzlemaker
- [ ] Fluency Solutions
- [ ] Listening Library

 Independent Practice

- [ ] Practice Book, 201–209
- [ ] Grammar Book, 116–120
- [ ] Spelling Book, 93–96

My To-Do List

✔ **Put a check next to the activities you complete.**

📖 Reading

- ☐ Time your reading
- ☐ Retell the story

Ⓐ︎Ⓑ︎Ⓒ︎ Word Work

- ☐ Build *er, ir, ur* words
- ☐ Sort words by letter patterns

✏️ Writing

- ☐ Write a flower poem
- ☐ Write about plant care

🔍 Science

- ☐ Label plant parts
- ☐ Write about a plant

🌎 Social Studies

- ☐ Draw a neighborhood garden
- ☐ Make a poster

📖 Leveled Readers

- ☐ Write About It!
- ☐ Content Connection

🖱️ Technology

- ☐ Buggles and Beezy
- ☐ Vocabulary Puzzlemaker
- ☐ Fluency Solutions
- ☐ Listening Library

🖌️ Independent Practice

- ☐ Practice Book, 210–218
- ☐ Grammar Book, 121–125
- ☐ Spelling Book, 97–100

My To-Do List

✔ **Put a check next to the activities you complete.**

📖 Reading

- [ ] Pick a book
- [ ] Read with a CD

✏️ Writing

- [ ] Draw a bug
- [ ] Write a bug song

🌎 Social Studies

- [ ] Draw a place with bugs
- [ ] Write about bugs

🖱️ Technology

- [ ] Buggles and Beezy
- [ ] Vocabulary Puzzlemaker
- [ ] Fluency Solutions
- [ ] Listening Library

Ⓐ Ⓑ Ⓒ Word Work

- [ ] Build words with *ou, ow*
- [ ] Sort *ou, ow* words

🔍 Science

- [ ] Write about bugs
- [ ] List area bugs

📖 Leveled Readers

- [ ] Write About It!
- [ ] Content Connection

Independent Practice

- [ ] Practice Book, 221–229
- [ ] Grammar Book, 126–130
- [ ] Spelling Book, 101–104

Name _____ Date _____

My To-Do List

✔ Put a check next to the activities you complete.

 Reading

☐ Pick a book
☐ Read along with a CD

 Word Work

☐ Build words with *oo*
☐ Sort words with *oo*

 Writing

☐ Draw yourself in space
☐ Write about health

 Science

☐ Write about a planet
☐ Find answers about planets

 Social Studies

☐ Draw Earth from space
☐ Find out what astronauts see in space

 Leveled Readers

☐ Write About It!
☐ Content Connection

 Technology

☐ Buggles and Beezy
☐ Vocabulary Puzzlemaker
☐ Fluency Solutions
☐ Listening Library

Independent Practice

☐ Practice Book, 230–238
☐ Grammar Book, 131–135
☐ Spelling Book, 105–108

My To-Do List

✔ Put a check next to the activities you complete.

 Reading

☐ Read a book
☐ Read with a CD

 Word Work

☐ Build *oo* words
☐ Sort *oo* words

 Writing

☐ Write about a job
☐ Write about a music job

 Science

☐ Draw a science job
☐ Write about being a scientist

 Social Studies

☐ Write about a helper
☐ Write about a worker

 Leveled Readers

☐ Write About It!
☐ Content Connection

Technology

☐ Buggles and Beezy
☐ Vocabulary Puzzlemaker
☐ Fluency Solutions
☐ Listening Library

 Independent Practice

☐ Practice Book, 239–247
☐ Grammar Book, 136–140
☐ Spelling Book, 109–112

© Macmillan/McGraw-Hill

My To-Do List

✔ **Put a check next to the activities you complete.**

📖 Reading

- ☐ Read a book
- ☐ Read with a CD

(ABC) Word Work

- ☐ Build words with /ô/ *au*, *aw*
- ☐ Sort words

✏️ Writing

- ☐ Draw and label pictures
- ☐ Write about animals staying healthy

🔍 Science

- ☐ Draw a baby animal
- ☐ Write about animals staying safe

🌎 Social Studies

- ☐ Draw water animals
- ☐ Write about land animals

📖 Leveled Readers

- ☐ Write About It!
- ☐ Content Connection

🖱️ Technology

- ☐ Buggles and Beezy
- ☐ Vocabulary Puzzlemaker
- ☐ Fluency Solutions
- ☐ Listening Library

✍️ Independent Practice

- ☐ Practice Book, 248–256
- ☐ Grammar Book, 141–145
- ☐ Spelling Book, 113–116

Name _____ Date _____

My To-Do List

✔ Put a check next to the activities you complete.

 Reading

☐ Pick a book
☐ Read along with a CD

 Word Work

☐ Build words with *oi, oy*
☐ Sort words

 Writing

☐ Draw and label pictures
☐ Write a poem

 Science

☐ Write about building from nature
☐ Draw things from nature

Social Studies

☐ Draw buildings
☐ Draw houses

 Leveled Readers

☐ Write About It!
☐ Content Connection

 Technology

☐ Buggles and Beezy
☐ Vocabulary Puzzlemaker
☐ Fluency Solutions
☐ Listening Library

 Independent Practice

☐ Practice Book, 257–265
☐ Grammar Book, 146–150
☐ Spelling Book, 117–120

Foldables™

by Dinah Zike

What are Foldables™?

Foldables are multi-dimensional graphic organizers that can be used for skills reinforcement, practice, and/or information organizing.

Why use Foldables™?

Not only do Foldables reinforce skills and strategies essential for reading success, they provide a kinesthetic tool for organizing and analyzing learning.

Dear Teacher,

A Foldable is a three-dimensional, student-made (and/or teacher-made) interactive graphic organizer based upon a skill. Making a Foldable gives students a fast, kinesthetic activity that helps them organize and retain information either before, during, or after reading. In this section of the *Teacher's Resource Book*, you will find instructions for making Foldables, as well as ideas on how to use them to reinforce and practice phonics, vocabulary, spelling, and comprehension skills.

In this section, you will find Foldables to help you
- replace photocopied activity sheets with student-generated print
- present content and skills in a clear, visual, kinesthetic format
- incorporate the use of such skills as comparing and contrasting, recognizing cause and effect, and finding similarities and differences
- assess student progress and learning levels
- immerse students in new and previously learned vocabulary and reading skills
- teach students unique ways to make study guides and practice materials, and
- provide students with a sense of ownership in their learning.

I am excited to hand these Foldable ideas and activities over to you and your students. Have fun using, adding to, and amending them to meet individual needs.

Sincerely,

Dinah Zike

Creating and Storing Foldables™

As you use the Foldables outlined in this *Teacher's Resource Book*, discuss with students how they can adapt them to make their own Foldables learning and study aids. Teach students to write—titles, vocabulary words, concepts, skills, questions, main ideas—on the front tabs of their Foldables. By doing this, key concepts are viewed every time a student looks at a Foldable. Foldables help students focus on and remember the information presented without being distracted by other print. Remind students to write more specific information—supporting ideas, examples of a concept, definitions, answers to questions, observations—under the tabs.

Turn one-gallon freezer bags into student portfolios and storage containers for Foldables.

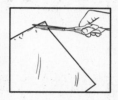 Cut the bottom corners off each bag so they won't hold air and will stack and store easily.

 Write student names across the top of the plastic portfolios with a permanent marker and cover the writing with two-inch clear tape to keep it from wearing off.

Place a piece of cardboard inside each portfolio to give it strength and to act as a divider.

 Store Foldables in a giant laundry soap box. Or, students can carry their portfolios in a three-ring binder if you place a strip of two-inch clear tape along one side and punch three holes through the taped edge.

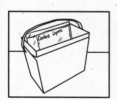

Foldables™
in this section

Basic Shapes... 37

Answer Mitt (with student copying master) 38

Accordion Book 40

Standing Cube 42

Layered Book 44

Large Word Study Book............................... 46

Matchbook 48

Two- and Three-tab 50

Three-tab Poster.. 52

Three- and Four-tab..................................... 54

Pocket... 56

Four-tab Word Study 58

Pyramid 60

Picture Frame 62

Foldables Correlated to Reading Skills.......... 64

Basic Shapes
by Dinah Zike

These figures illustrate the basic folds that are referred to throughout the following section of this book.

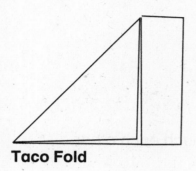

Taco Fold

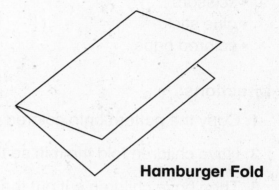

Hamburger Fold

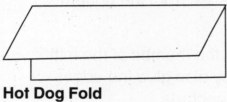
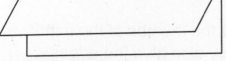

Hot Dog Fold

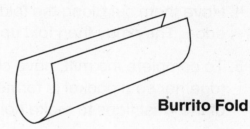

Burrito Fold

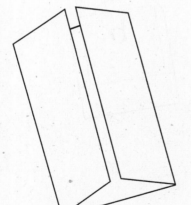

Shutter Fold

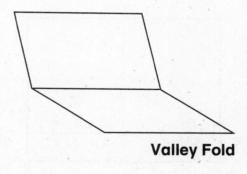

Valley Fold

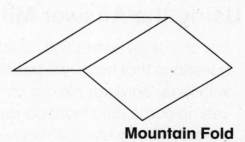

Mountain Fold

Foldables

Answer Mitt Foldable™

by Dinah Zike

Materials:
- Copying Master on page 39
- scissors
- glue stick
- colored paper

Directions:

1. Copy the pattern onto colored paper.

2. Have children fold the mitt so the fingertips touch each other.

3. Then have children cut out the mitt shape.

4. Have them cut along the fold an inch or so in from the bottom edge. They may then fold up the flaps.

5. To complete the mitt, have children glue the thumbs of the mitt together so a pocket is formed. They may also glue the edges of the wrist flaps to make holders for letter cards.

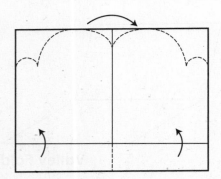 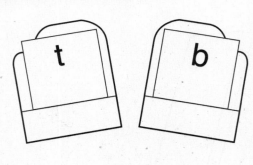

Using the Answer Mitt Foldable™

For any skills instruction, children can use the mitt to answer questions that have two possible responses. The mitt can be used with letter cards or picture cards (from pages 66–87 of this book), yes/no cards, and word cards (from pages 90–149 of this book). When children use the Answer Mitt Foldable in whole class or small group instruction, you will be better able to monitor their progress.

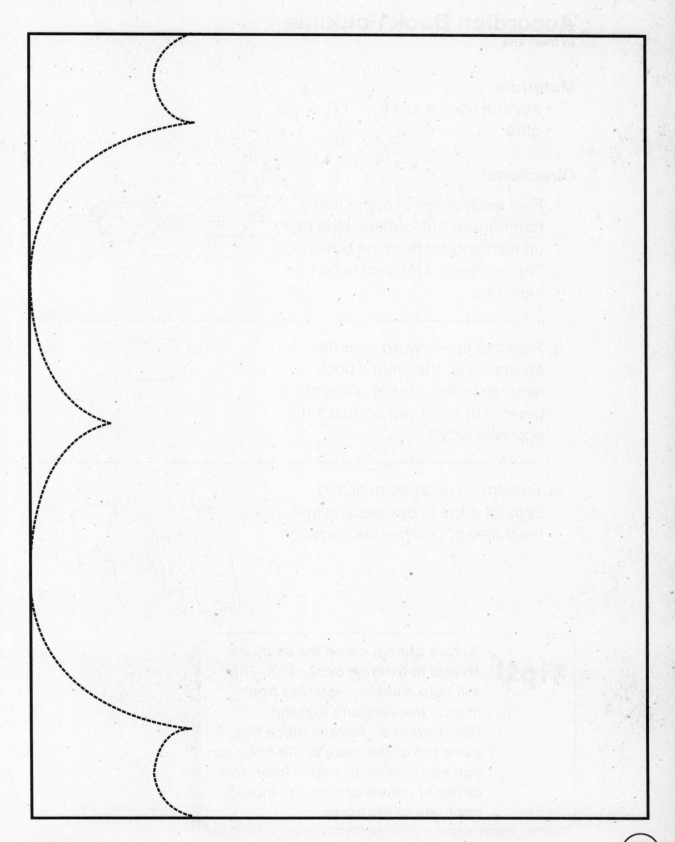

Foldables

Accordion Book Foldable™

by Dinah Zike

Materials:
- several sheets of 11″ × 17″ paper
- glue

Directions:

1. Fold each sheet of paper into a hamburger, but fold one side half an inch shorter than the other side. This will form a tab that is half an inch long.

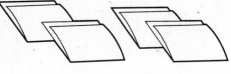

2. Fold this tab forward over the shorter side, then fold it back away from the shorter piece of paper. (In other words, fold it the opposite way.)

3. To form an accordion, glue a straight edge of one section into the valley of another section's tab.

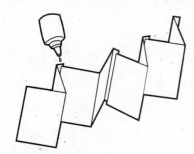

Tips! *Before gluing, stand the sections on end to form an accordion. This will help children visualize how to glue the sections together (illustration 3). Always place the extra tab at the back of the book so you can add more pages later. Use different colors of paper to indicate sections of the book.*

Using the Accordion Book Foldable™
by Dinah Zike

Vocabulary/Vocabulary Strategy Application
Use the Accordion Book Foldable to create vocabulary concept books for topics such as:

- Shapes
- Colors
- Position words
- Number words
- Word categories (such as food words, weather words, etc.)

Phonemic Awareness/Phonics Application
Use the accordion book to create a letter-sound book or an alphabet book. The book can also be used to collect and share single letter-sound examples.

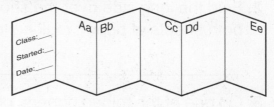

Comprehension Application
The accordion book is perfect for post-reading skills application. Use the book to record text sequence (first, next, last) or plot sequence (beginning, middle, end). Try color-coding each section so children can see the sequence clearly.

Children may wish to use this Foldable for publishing their own stories.

Grammar Application
Like the vocabulary word categories application above, the accordion book can be used to collect and share grammar skills such as:

- Nouns (proper nouns, common nouns)
- Action verbs
- Adjectives

Storage Notes

Display in a workstation, center, or library corner. Store by slipping it into a binder.

Foldables

Standing Cube Foldable™
by Dinah Zike

Materials:
- two sheets of 11" × 17" paper
- glue

Directions:

1. Fold each sheet like a hamburger, but fold one side one-half inch shorter than the other side.

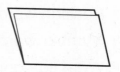

2. Fold the long side over the short side on both sheets of paper, making tabs.

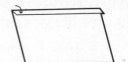

3. On one of the folded papers, place a small amount of glue along the tab, next to the valley but not in it.

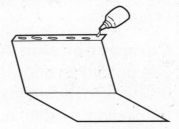

4. Place the non-folded edge of the second sheet of paper square into the valley and fold the glue-covered tab over this sheet of paper. Press flat until the glue holds. Repeat with the other side.

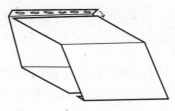

5. Allow the glue to dry completely before continuing. After the glue has dried, the cube can be collapsed flat to allow children to work on the content.

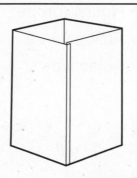

Foldables

Using the Standing Cube Foldable™
by Dinah Zike

Vocabulary Application
Use the Foldable for developing vocabulary concepts with children. Each side of the cube can show information about a word (definition, example sentences, picture, etc.).

Phonemic Awareness/Phonics Application

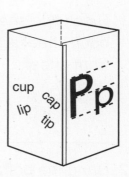

With the class, create a Foldable for each letter of the alphabet. Have children help by providing the content for each side: pictures whose names begin with the letter sound (use the picture cards on pages 66–87), words that begin or end with the letter-sound, and handwriting models for capital and lowercase letters.

Comprehension Application

Have children work in small groups to create a Foldable about a story character they are studying. Each side of the Foldable should illustrate or tell about character traits.

Grammar Application
Use the Foldable to collect and share types of nouns or adjectives.

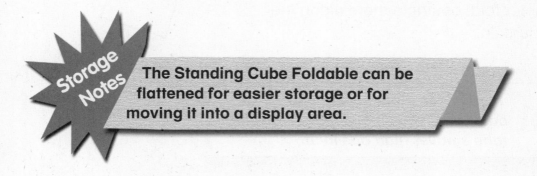

Storage Notes

The Standing Cube Foldable can be flattened for easier storage or for moving it into a display area.

Layered Book Foldable™
by Dinah Zike

Materials:
- two sheets of 8½″ × 11″ paper
- glue

Directions:

1. Stack two sheets of paper so that the back sheet is one inch higher than the front sheet.

2. Bring the bottom of both sheets upward and align the edges so that all of the layers or tabs are the same distance apart.

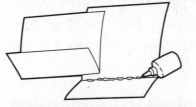

3. When all tabs are an equal distance apart, fold the papers and crease well.

4. Open the papers and glue them together along the valley, or inner center fold, or staple them along the mountain.

Tip! *If you need more layers, use additional sheets of paper. Make the tabs smaller than one inch.*

Foldables

Using the Layered Book Foldable™

by Dinah Zike

Vocabulary Application

Have children create this Foldable to help them review vocabulary words. Have them write a word on each tab and then flip the tab to draw a picture or write the definition. The same thing can be done with antonyms and synonyms.

Phonemic Awareness/Phonics Application

A review/study guide of vowel and consonant sounds can be done with this Foldable. For example:

- Vowels
- *r*-controlled vowels
- digraphs (*th, wh, sh, ch*)

Vowels
a
e
i
o
u

Comprehension Application

Use the Foldable to aid in the following skills reinforcement:

- Character study (one tab per story character)
- Retelling
- Asking Questions

Character Study
Big Bear
Middle Bear
Small Bear
Goldilocks

Study Skills and Grammar Applications

This Foldable can be used to review/reinforce concepts studied.

Foldables

Large Word Study Book Foldable™

by Dinah Zike

Materials:

- several sheets of 11" × 17" paper (one sheet for each word studied)
- stapler

Directions:

1. Fold each sheet like a hot dog, but fold one side one inch shorter than the other side.

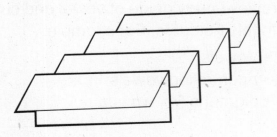

2. Stack the sheets so the folds are side by side.

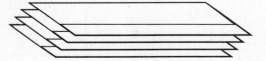

3. Staple sheets together along the tabbed end (the bottom of the pages).

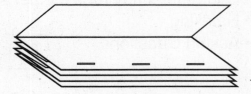

Using the Large Word Study Book Foldable™
by Dinah Zike

Vocabulary and Phonics/Spelling Applications

With a small group, make a Foldable for word study/review. Display the book in a workstation for repeated review. The size and the format also make it easy for you and children to use them as lap flashcards.

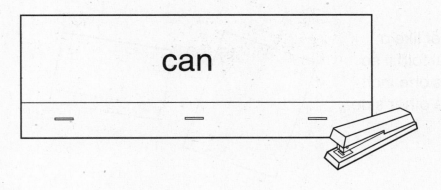

can

I <u>can</u> run fast.
We <u>can</u> go home.
<u>Can</u> we go play?

Storage Notes Collect and use these books through the year. Store each book in a labeled legal-size folder.

Foldables

Matchbook Foldable™ Bulletin Board

by Dinah Zike

Materials:
- several sheets of 8½" × 11" paper
- staples or thumbtacks
- bulletin board

Directions:

1. Fold each sheet like a hamburger, but fold it so that one side is one inch longer than the other side.

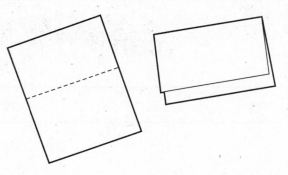

2. Fold the one-inch tab over the short side to form an envelope-like fold.

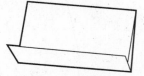

3. After the content has been added to the front and inside, post the Foldable on a bulletin board.

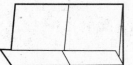

Using the Matchbook Foldable™ Bulletin Board
by Dinah Zike

Vocabulary Application
With children, create Foldables for weekly vocabulary. Write the vocabulary word on the front. Have children draw a picture and dictate a sentence for the inside.

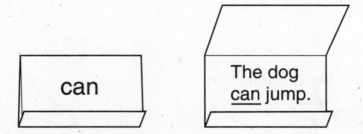

Phonemic Awareness/Phonics/Spelling Application
Use the Foldable for review of phonics and/or spelling words.

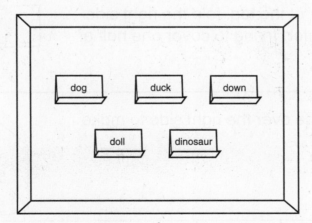

Comprehension Application
This Foldable works for reinforcing skills such as:
- Cause and effect
- Making predictions

Foldables

Two- and Three-tab Foldable™

by Dinah Zike

Several options adapt this Foldable to initial, medial, and final letter-sound review.

Materials:
- 8½″ × 11″ sheet of paper
- scissors

Directions:

1. Fold the sheet like a hamburger.

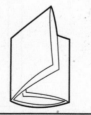

2. With the paper horizontal and the fold of the hamburger at the top, fold the right side toward the center, trying to cover one half of the paper.

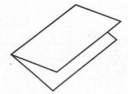

3. Fold the left side over the right side to make three sections.

4. Open the right and left folds. Place one hand between the two thicknesses of paper and cut up the two valleys so there are three tabs.

Using the Two- and Three-tab Foldable™
by Dinah Zike

Phonics/Spelling Application

Use the Three-Tab Foldable as an alternate to Sound Boxes. Open the tabs and write a CVC word on the bottom paper so that one letter is shown in each box. Have children practice blending and decoding words.

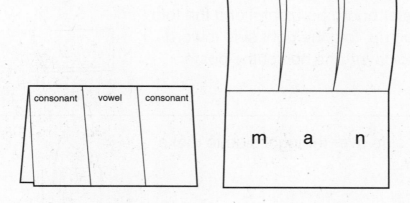

Another option is to cut off one of the tabs so that the Foldable has two tabs. After step 4, cut off the first tab. Open the other two tabs and write a CVC word on the bottom paper so that one letter is shown in each box. For further practice with letter-sound blending, fold the tabs over to make another CVC word for decoding.

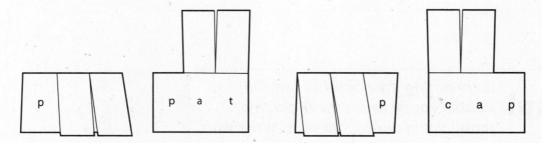

Foldables

Three-tab Poster Foldable™
by Dinah Zike

Materials:
- large poster board

Directions:

1. Fold poster board like a hot dog.

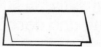

_____

2. With the poster board horizontal and the fold of the hot dog up, fold the right side toward the center, to cover one half of the poster board.

_____

3. Fold the left side over the right side to make three sections.

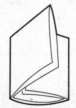

_____

4. Open the folds. Place one hand between the two thicknesses of the poster board and cut up the two valleys on the top flap. This will create three tabs.

Tip! *Laminating the poster board will enable you to reuse this Foldable many times during the year. Write with a dry erase marker.*

Foldables

Using the Three-tab Poster Foldable™
by Dinah Zike

Comprehension Application
This Foldable may be adapted and used to create the following graphic organizers:

- Venn Diagram
- K-W-L Chart

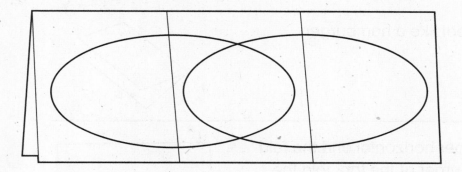

What I Know	What I Want to Know	What I Learned

Three- and Four-tab Foldable™
by Dinah Zike

Several options adapt this Foldable to digraph, blend, and vowel variant letter-sound review.

Materials:
- one 8½" × 11" sheet of paper
- scissors

Directions:

1. Fold the sheet like a hamburger.

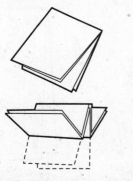

2. With the paper horizontal and the fold of the hamburger at the top, fold the hamburger into four vertical sections.

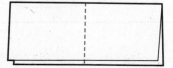
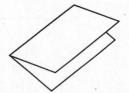

3. Open these folds. Place one hand between the folded hamburger and cut up the three valleys so there are four tabs.

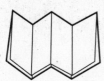

Using the Three- and Four-tab Foldable™

by Dinah Zike

Phonics/Spelling Application

Use the Four-Tab Foldable as an alternate to Sound Boxes. Open the tabs and write a CCVC word on the bottom paper so that one letter is shown in each box. Have children practice blending and decoding words.

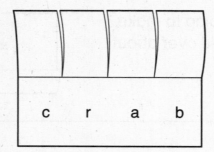

Another option is to make the Foldable with three tabs. After step 2, cut only the first and the third valleys. Open all three tabs and write a word with a vowel digraph, such as *ow*, on the bottom paper, so that the middle tab covers the vowel digraph.

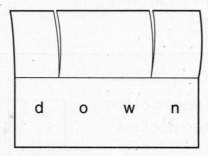

Or, cut only the first and second tabs and write a word that ends with double letters or the digraph *-ck*.

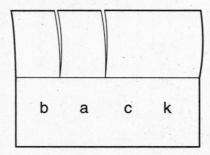

Foldables

Pocket Foldable™

by Dinah Zike

Materials:
- one 11" × 17" sheet of paper
- glue

Directions:

1. Begin as if you are going to make a hot dog, but only fold over about three inches.

2. With the paper horizontal and the fold on the bottom, fold the right side toward the center, trying to cover one half of the paper. Then, fold the left side over the right side to make three sections.

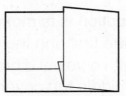

3. Glue the right and left edges of the original fold so that three pockets are created.

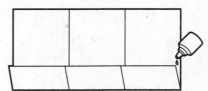

Using the Pocket Foldable™
by Dinah Zike

Vocabulary and Phonics/Spelling Applications

Have children use this Foldable as a study aid. Copies of word cards (see pages 90–149 in this book) can be sorted and stored by children as they learn words. Help children label the pockets as shown below. As they study the words, have them move the cards to the appropriate pockets.

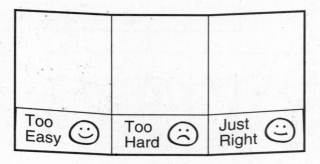

Tip! *Send this Foldable home with children so they can review and sort words with family members.*

Storage Notes Heavy stock paper will improve durability. Post the Foldable on a board for use during workstation time.

Foldables

Four-tab Word Study Foldable™

by Dinah Zike

Materials:
- one 11" × 17" sheet of paper
- scissors

Directions:

1. Fold the sheet like a hot dog, but fold it so that one side is one inch longer than the other side.

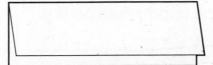

2. With the paper horizontal and the fold of the hot dog at the top, fold the hot dog into four (or more depending upon how many words are to be studied) vertical sections.

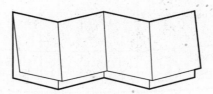

3. Open these folds. Place one hand between the sides of the folded hot dog and cut up the three valleys so there are four tabs.

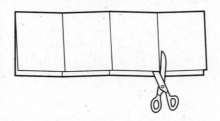

4. Turn the Foldable so it can be used vertically.

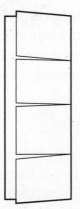

Using the Four-tab Word Study Foldable™
by Dinah Zike

Vocabulary and Phonics/Spelling Applications

Have children use this Foldable as a study aid. Have them write a vocabulary or spelling word on a tab, then open the tab, draw a picture, write a definition, or write a sample sentence.

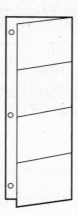

© Macmillan/McGraw-Hill

Storage Notes Punch holes on flaps to compile word lists in a binder. Heavy stock paper will improve durability.

Pyramid Foldable™

by Dinah Zike

Materials:
- one 8½" × 11" sheet of paper
- scissors
- glue

Directions:

1. Fold the sheet into a taco. Cut off the excess rectangular tab formed by the fold.

2. Open the folded taco and refold it like a taco the opposite way to create an X-fold.

3. Cut one of the valleys to the center of the X, or the midpoint, and stop. This forms two triangular flaps.

4. Glue one of the flaps under the other, forming a pyramid.

Tip! *Use this Foldable with data occurring in threes.*

Using the Pyramid Foldable™
by Dinah Zike

Vocabulary Application
The Pyramid Foldable can be used to sort and review concepts studied, such as sequence words or words with inflectional endings (-s, -es, -ies).

Phonics/Spelling Application
Children can sort words into three categories. Some examples:

- Initial (or final) consonants (such as *p, m, s*)
- Short vowels (such as *a, e, i*)
- Long vowels (such as *o_e, oa, o*)
- Blends (*sl, st, sw*)

Comprehension Application
Not only can children use the pyramid to record information about what they read, they can do it in a few different ways. With one pyramid they can do things such as the following:

- Compare three different story characters
- Create a K-W-L chart
- Record information about story beginning, middle, and end

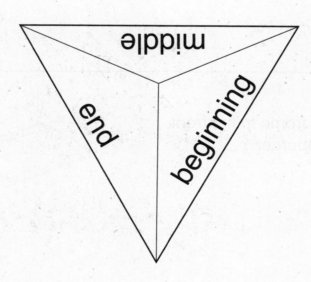

Picture Frame Foldable™
by Dinah Zike

Materials:
- one sheet of 8½" × 11" paper in a bright color
- one sheet of 11" × 17" paper
- scissors
- glue

Directions:

1. Fold the 8½" × 11" paper into a hot dog.

_____

2. Starting at the fold, cut a frame shape (as illustrated). Set aside.

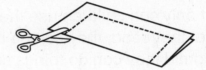

_____

3. Fold the 11" × 17" paper into a hamburger.

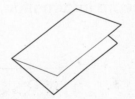

_____

4. Glue the paper frame to the front side of the hamburger.

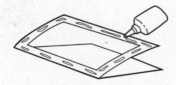

Using the Picture Frame Foldable™
by Dinah Zike

Vocabulary and Phonics/Spelling Applications
Children can glue pictures or draw pictures in the frame to reinforce a vocabulary word or concept. On the inside of the book, they can write or dictate sentences about the word or concept.

Comprehension Application
To reinforce character study, have children illustrate a story character (or use story character patterns on pages 196–226 of this book) and write or dictate sentences about the character. The same sort of activity can be done with the following skills:

- Setting/plot
- Main idea/details
- Retelling a scene

Grammar Application
Have children use the frame to illustrate a noun or a verb. Then have them write or dictate sentences about the word.

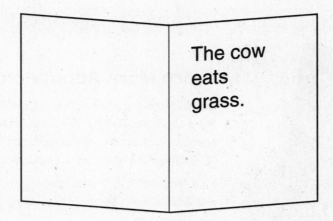

The cow eats grass.

Correlated to Reading Skills

Foldable	Phonics/Phonemic Awareness/Spelling	Vocabulary (including Oral Vocabulary)	Vocabulary Strategies	Comprehension	Study Skills	Grammar
Answer Mitt	X	X	X	X	X	X
Accordion Book	X	X	X	X		X
Standing Cube	X	X		X		X
Layered Book	X	X		X	X	X
Large Word Study Book	X	X				
Matchbook	X	X		X		
Two- and Three-tab	X					
Three-tab Poster				X		
Three- and Four-tab	X					
Pocket	X	X				
Four-tab Word Study	X	X				
Pyramid	X			X		
Picture Frame				X		X

Learn More About Foldables™

Dinah Zike is the author of more than 150 educational books and materials. For a catalog of Dinah's current publications, as well as information on her keynotes and teacher workshops, call 1-800-99DINAH (1-800-993-4624), or visit her Web site at www.dinah.com.

Look for *Dinah Zike's Big Book of Phonics, Vocabulary, and Spelling* with 260 full-color pages of Foldable activities and word lists for the K–6 classroom.

Look for other practical and inexpensive storage, display, and organization ideas in *Dinah Zike's Classroom Organization: It Can Be Done*. This newly revised and updated publication is perfect for the K–6 classroom teacher who needs to get organized.

Word Study

Use the pages in this section to offer further practice with phonics, spelling, and word meanings.

Picture Cards **66**
- illustrations of words with key vowel and consonant sounds

Alphabet Letter Cards **88**
- lowercase and capital letter cards
- use for phonics and spelling games and activities

Spelling Word Cards **90**
- reproducible cards for each week's words
- tested, review, and challenge words
- key words for sorting activities

Vocabulary Word Cards **120**
- reproducible cards for each week's tested words
- blank cards for additional words

Sound Boxes **150**
- three- and four-part boxes
- use with letter cards for phonics and spelling practice

Games **152**
- *Learning with Games* – suggestions for games that support word study strategies, dictionary skills, and comprehension skills
- boards, grids, spinners, and other ideas to customize for your class

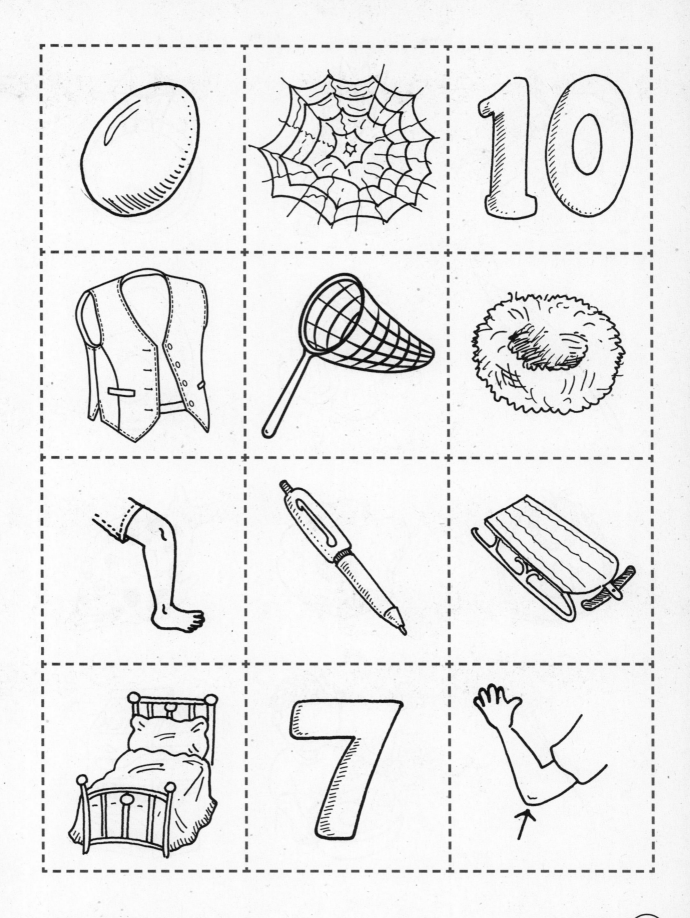

Short i

Picture Cards

Short u

Picture Cards

Picture Cards

© Macmillan/McGraw-Hill

Consonant Blends

Picture Cards

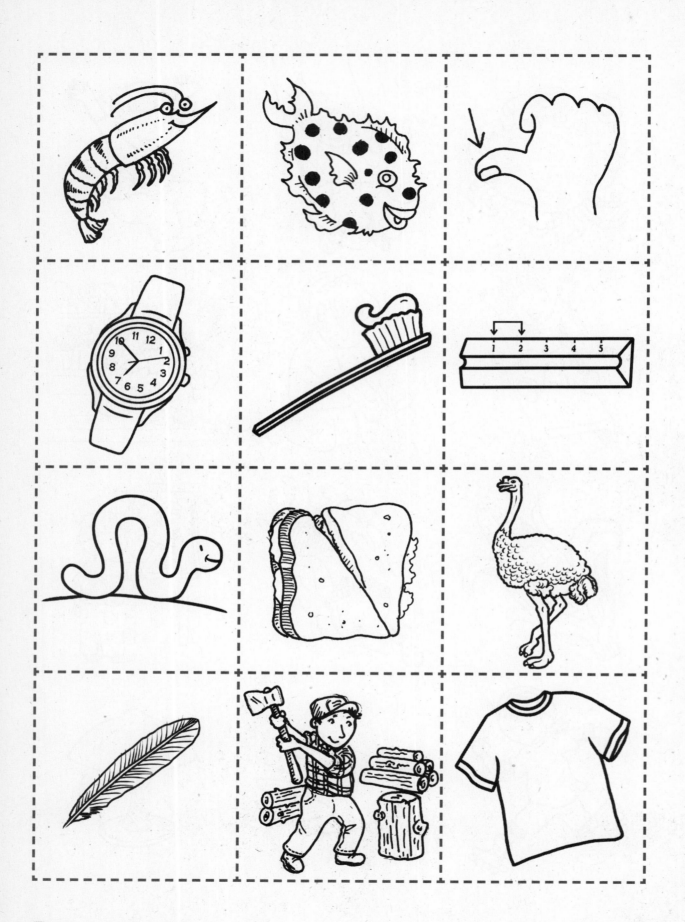

Consonant Digraphs

Picture Cards

Long i

Picture Cards

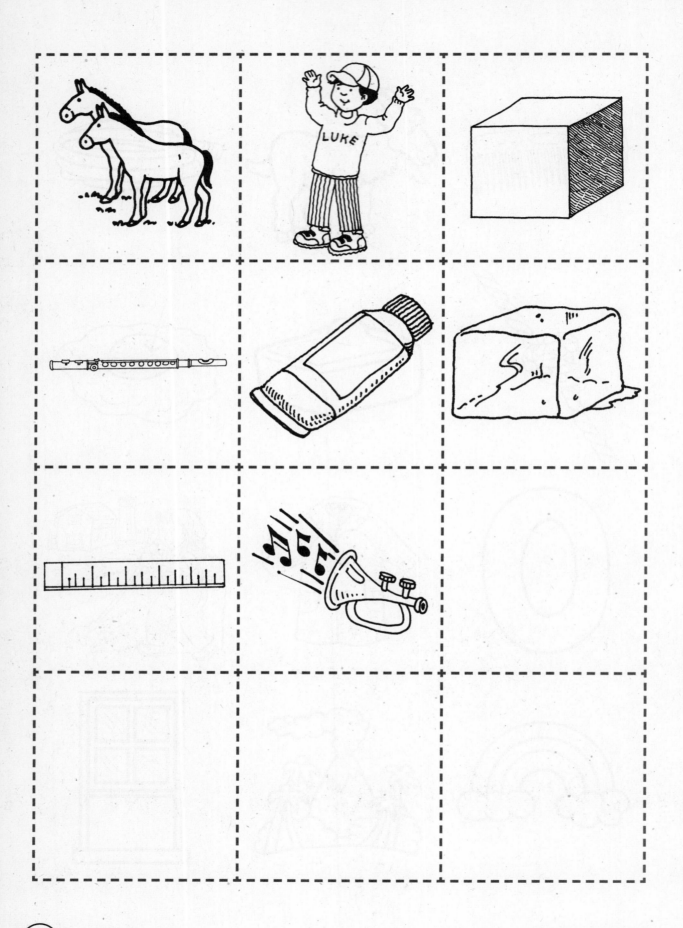

Picture Cards

Assorted Long Vowels　(81)

Vowel Variants

Picture Cards

a	b	c	d	e
f	g	h	i	j
k	l	m	n	o
p	q	r	s	t
u	v	w	x	y
z				

Letter Cards

A B C D E

F G H I J

K L M N O

P Q R S T

U V W X Y

Z

Letter Cards

-at	-an
sat	tan
man	cat
hat	mat
ran	can
up	down

Spelling Word Cards

-ad	**-ap**
-ack	**bad**
lap	**tack**
dad	sad
back	nap
tap	sack
too	over
man	mat

-in	-it
-iss	hiss
kit	bin
pin	win
hit	sit
miss	kiss
be	ride
sad	map

Spelling Word Cards

cr-	gr-
tr-	crib
crab	grab
grass	trap
trip	that
good	hit
win	

-nd	-st
-nt	**-nk**
sand	**hand**
trip	**vest**
ant	land
very	fast
grass	sink
	help
	west

-op	**-og**
-ot	**pop**
fog	**pot**
hop	top
log	hog
hot	lot
one	they
sand	sink

-eg	-en
-et	peg
den	pet
leg	beg
men	hen
let	get
who	some
hop	hot

sh	th
mash	**think**
fish	shop
ship	with
thin	thank
lives	many
beg	get

-un	**-ut**
-ug	**sun**
but	**hug**
run	fun
nut	cut
bug	rug
under	put
thin	shop

cl-	fl-
bl-	**blink**
clap	**flap**
clip	clock
flag	flip
black	block
school	today
fun	nut

© Macmillan/McGraw-Hill

-ake	**-ame**
-ate	**cake**
same	**date**
make	take
came	game
gate	late
walk	all
black	flag

sl-	**sn-**
sp-	**slap**
snip	**spot**
sled	slip
snake	snap
spill	spin
people	water
make	game

ch	**-tch**
wh-	**when**
pitch	**chest**
whip	whale
catch	match
chin	chop
our	your
slip	spin

-ike	**-ide**
-ine	**Mike**
side	**fine**
like	spike
ride	hide
bike	mine
call	there
whip	chop

str-	spl-
scr-	stripe
scrape	splint
strike	string
splash	split
scrub	scrap
says	were
like	ride

Spelling Word Cards

-oke	**-ose**
-ote	**poke**
rose	**quote**
joke	woke
nose	hose
note	vote
every	any
splash	string

-une	**-use**
-ute	**-ule**
use	June
tune	flute
cute	mule
done	after
woke	nose

ay	ai
mail	rain
chain	way
play	day
great	know
cute	use

e	ee
ea	**he**
seem	**team**
me	we
feed	keep
seat	beak
friends	knew
main	day

Spelling Word Cards

-py	**-ny**
-dy	**sunny**
happy	**handy**
bumpy	penny
puppy	sandy
funny	bunny
before	heard
keep	seat

o	**oa**
ow	**yolk**
soap	**elbow**
road	**mow**
low	row
boat	coat
no	go
mother	father
puppy	funny

i	y
igh	**wild**
dry	**tight**
find	kind
night	right
by	my
never	head
low	boat

-art	-arn
-arm	cart
art	barn
yarn	arm
harm	better
children	right
by	

-orn	-ork
worn	**stork**
born	corn
cork	fork
horn	pork
nothing	thought
barn	art

er	ir
ur	girl
nurse	under
her	fern
bird	dirt
fur	burn
from	beautiful
fork	corn

Spelling Word Cards

ou	ow
house	**now**
cow	how
town	out
mouse	mouth
gone	been
her	burn

-ook	-ood
hook	**good**
book	took
look	hood
cook	wood
Earth	bear
town	mouth

-ool	-oom
-oon	**tool**
spoon	**groom**
broom	room
pool	cool
soon	moon
laugh	ever
hood	took

au	aw
pause	**jaw**
haul	claw
cause	paw
saw	dawn
air	enough
cool	soon

oi	**oy**
boil	**soy**
joy	toy
boy	spoil
coin	join
toward	circle
dawn	cause

down	not
jump	up

Vocabulary Word Cards

it	too
over	**yes**

Vocabulary Word Cards

Unit 1 • I Can! Can You? (121)

be

run

ride

| come | on |
| good | that |

help	use
now	**very**

Vocabulary Word Cards

does	they
her	two
one	

eat	some
no	who
of	

into	many
live	out

make	three
put	under
show	want

Vocabulary Word Cards

away	today
late	way
school	why

all	oh
could	pull
hello	walk

Vocabulary Word Cards

boy	together
care	water
girl	when
people	

again

would

light

your

our

Vocabulary Word Cards

call	more
funny	so
how	there

about	say
read	were
give	says

any	saw
every	soon
floating	sparkled
opened	

after	new
creation	old
done	terrific
find	work

Vocabulary Word Cards

cold	predict
extreme	sound
great	warm
know	their

by	house
curious	idea
far	kind
friends	knew

before	happen
began	haste
falls	heard
glared	told

always	mother
father	supposed
firm	try
love	

ball	never
head	perhaps
laughter	should
meadow	shout

Vocabulary Word Cards

better	machine
children	or
discovery	round

along	nothing
early	suddenly
errand	thought
instead	

animals	ground
beautiful	part
crowded	places
from	tiny

© Macmillan/McGraw-Hill

been	invisible
clues	other
gone	searching

bear	guess
birds	helmet
Earth	space
fooling	table

Vocabulary Word Cards

ever	laugh
goes	only
interesting	ordinary

across	**eyes**
air	**learn**
cub	**wild**
enough	

Vocabulary Word Cards

circle	toward
grew	welcoming
leave	wreck
toppled	

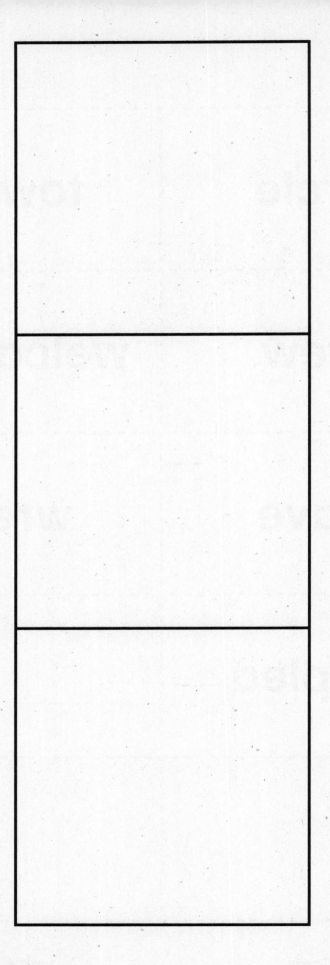

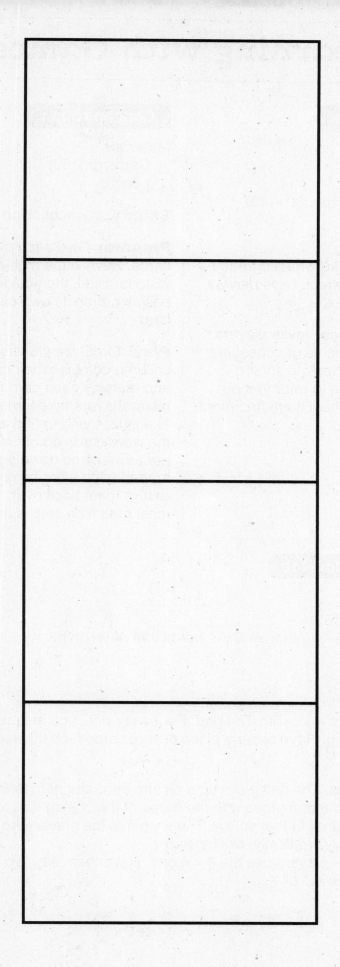

Learning with Games

Short o Word Maker

Materials
Word Wheel (p. 158)
pencils
Spelling Word Cards (pp. 90–119)

Skill: short o words

Prepare: Provide a word wheel for each player. On the outside wheel, have players write *ot*.

Play: On the inside wheel, invite players to write as many consonants or consonant blends as they can to complete short o words. Players may want to refer to their Spelling Word Cards to help them find more words.

Concentration

Materials
Cards (p. 159)
pencils

Skill: word recognition

Prepare: Give each player a copy of the cards. Review the high-frequency words or word families, then guide children to write each word on its own card. Cut out each card.

Play: Organize players into pairs. Have children combine their cards into one pile and then lay each card face down on the table. Players take turns choosing two cards at a time, trying to find a matching pair. If the word cards do not match, then the cards are turned face down again. Remind players to read each word before they collect them or turn them back over. The player with the most matching sets is the winner.

Rhyming Word Tic-Tac-Toe

Materials
Tic-Tac-Toe grid (p. 160)
Picture Cards (pp. 66–87; choose CVC words that have rhymes)
pencils

Skill: rhyming words

Prepare: Give partners a Tic-Tac-Toe grid. For easier use, you may want to enlarge the board while photocopying. Have players place picture cards face down on each space of the game board.

Play: Players take turns. The first picks up a picture card and names the picture. Then he or she has to say a word that rhymes with the name of the object. If successful, that player can then place an O or an X in that space. The winner is the player who first gets three Os or Xs in a row horizontally, vertically, or diagonally.

For a challenge, have players use the 4 x 4 grid. Have them say two rhyming words before they can place their O or X.

What Comes Next?

Materials

Puzzle Pieces, three pieces (p. 164)
crayons
scissors

Skill: Beginning, Middle, and End

Prepare: Tell each player to think of their favorite fairy tale or nursery rhyme. Give each player a copy of the three interlocking puzzle pieces. Have players draw a picture on each puzzle piece to show the beginning, middle, and end of their favorite story. Then each player cuts his or her puzzle pieces apart.

Play: Ask players to exchange their puzzle pieces with a partner. The partner will first put the puzzle pieces back together and then guess the story that is illustrated. Switch roles and repeat.

Sound Bingo

Materials

5 x 5 grid (one per player; p. 162)
4 x 4 grid (optional; p. 161)
game markers
Letter Cards (pp. 88–89)
pencils

Skill: letter/sound recognition

Prepare: Give players a grid and game markers. Pick alphabet letters from the Word-Building Letter Cards. Ask a volunteer to say the sound of the chosen letter. Players then write the letter onto their grid. Continue until all of the squares are filled.

Play: Play bingo by calling out various letter sounds. Players place markers on the corresponding letters. Play until one player has five markers in a row vertically, horizontally, or diagonally. You may use the 4 x 4 grid for a shorter game.

Letter Slip and Slide

Materials

Slip Strips (p. 163)
Spinner (p. 155)
pencils

Skill: decoding words with short o

Prepare: Organize players into groups of three. Give each player a copy of the slip strips. Have them write *ock* in the rectangular space to the right of the slots.
   Then have each small group make a spinner. Write the following consonants and consonant blends evenly around the spinner: *d, j, l, m, r, s, t, cl, st, fl, sm.*

Play: Each player spins the spinner and writes the letter onto his or her sliding strip until there are four different consonants or consonant blends on each strip. Players then take turns decoding and reading the words they have created using their letter slip and slide.

The Long Ride

Materials
   Oval board (p. 156)
   4-part spinner (p. 155)
   Letter Cards (b, h, k, p, r, s, t, w; p. 88)

Skill: recognizing short i

Prepare: Two or three players can play this game. Copy the oval game board. Draw a star in one square to indicate the beginning and ending point and the following endings on the board in an alternating pattern: _id, _it, _ip.

   Also give each group a 4-part spinner numbered with 0, 1, 2, and 3.

Play: The first player spins the spinner and moves his or her marker the number of spaces indicated. Then that player chooses an alphabet card and looks at the word ending in the square. The player reads the word he or she has created. If a nonsense word is created, the player continues choosing letter cards until a real word is made. The game continues until each player has been around the oval twice.

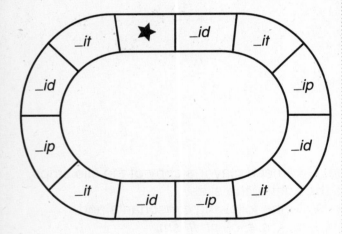

Read the Room Game

Materials
   S-shaped board (p. 157)
   4-part spinner (p. 155)
   game markers

Skill: high-frequency word recognition

Prepare: This game is for two players. Copy the S-shaped board for each pair. Label the first square *begin* and the last square *end*. Fill in the remaining squares with high-frequency words such as *and, are, do, for, go, has, have, he, here, is, like, little, look, me, my, play, said, see, she, to, the, this, was, we, what, where, with, you*.

   Give each pair a 4-part spinner filled in with the numbers 1, 2, 3, and 4.

Play: Each player spins the spinner and moves the number of spaces indicated. The player then reads the high-frequency word on which he or she has landed. Once the player has read the word on the board, then both players look around the room for the word. The first player to find the word spins the spinner. If neither player can find the word then the other player goes next. The winner is the player who reaches the *end* square first.

Games

Spinners

1. Cut out and complete a spinner.

2. Mount it on heavy paper.

3. Attach arrow with brad.

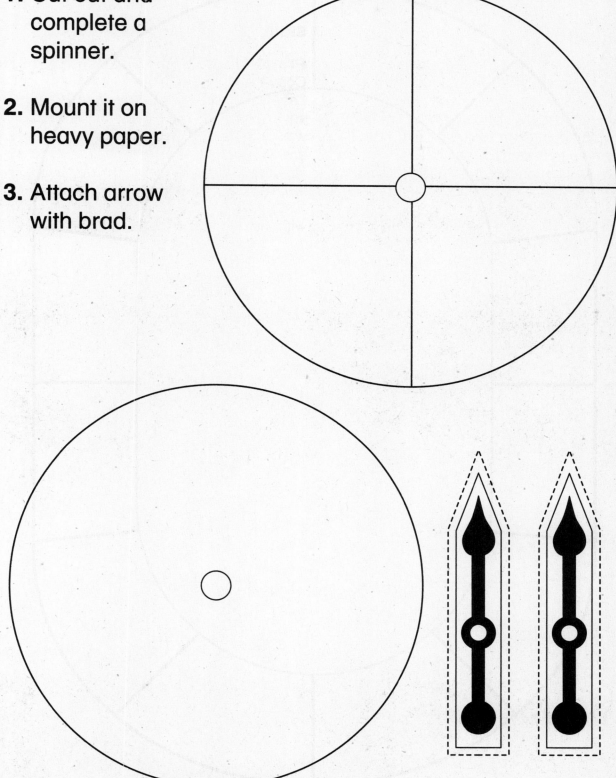

Oval Game Board

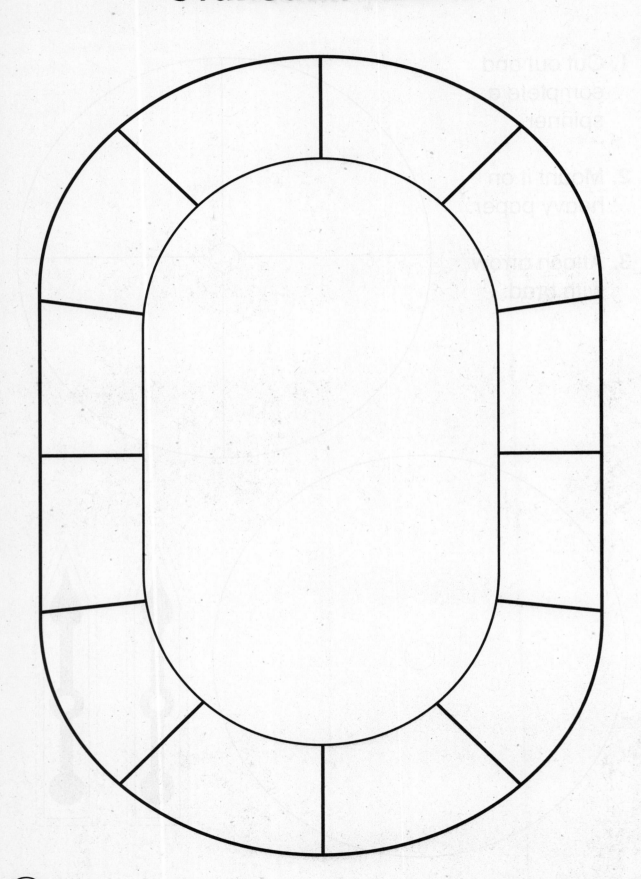

Games

S-shaped Game Board

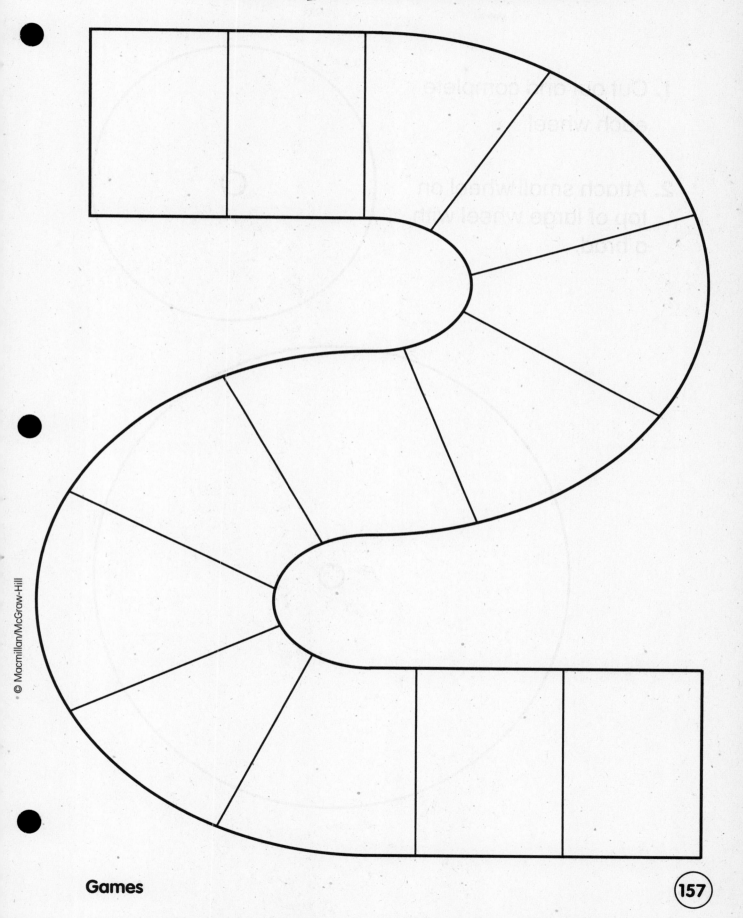

Games

Word Wheel

1. Cut out and complete each wheel.

2. Attach small wheel on top of large wheel with a brad.

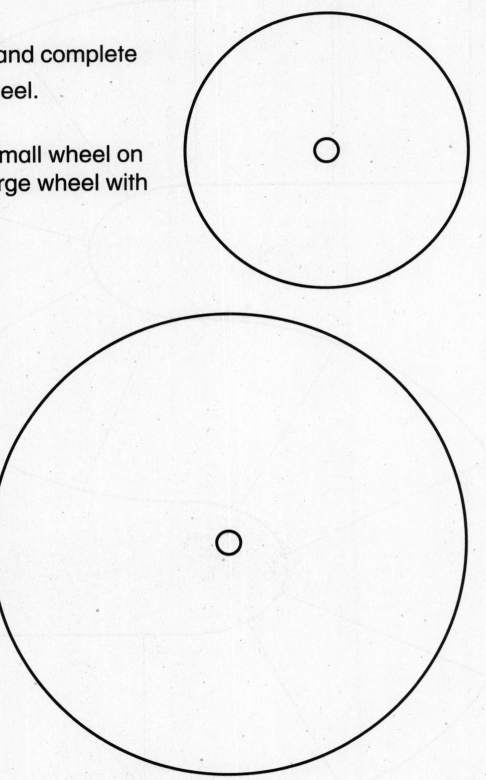

Games

Cards

Tic-Tac-Toe

4x4 Grid

5x5 Grid

Slip Strips

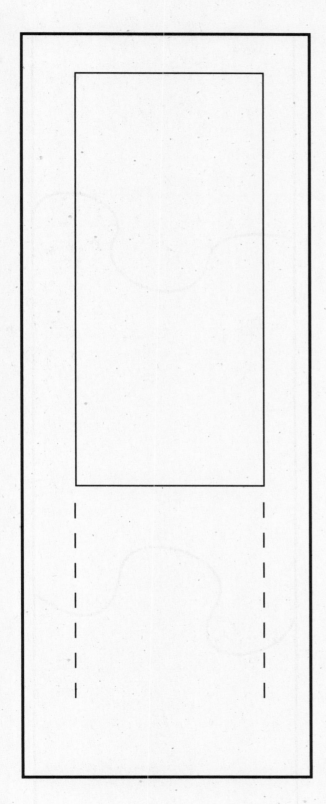

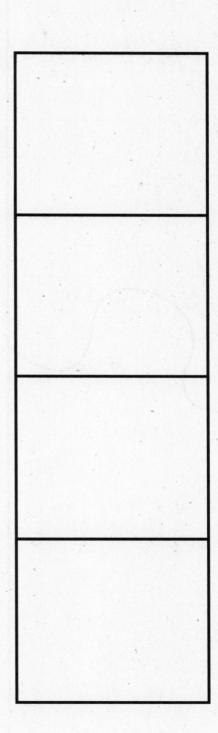

Puzzle Pieces

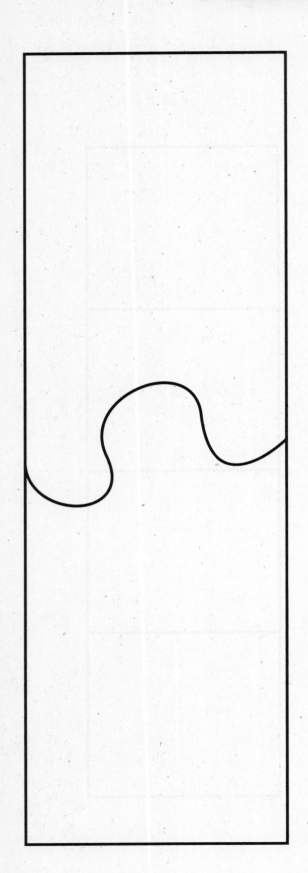
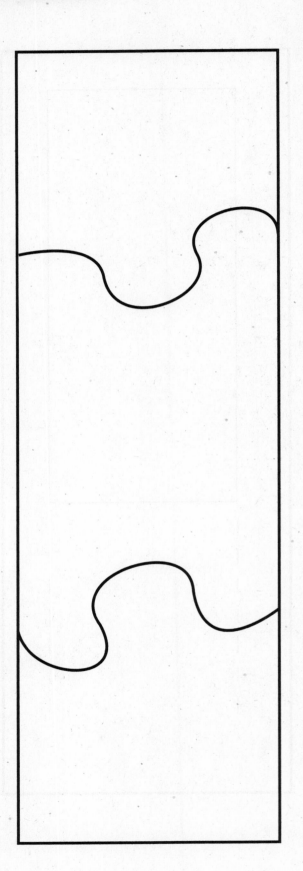

Additional Literacy Support

Use the pages in this section to support reading, writing, handwriting, listening, and speaking activities.

Rhymes and Chimes 166
• illustrated poems that support phonemic awareness

Story Patterns 196
• illustrations of characters for retelling main selections

Reader Response Sheets 227
• forms for fiction, non-fiction, and poetry

Writer's Checklists 230
• checklists for use with fiction and nonfiction writing

Proofreading Marks 232
• common proofreading marks to post or hand out

Writing Rubric 233
• four-point rubric to customize with the class

Picture Prompts 234
• *Writing to Picture Prompts* – tips on using the prompts for writing and test preparation
• prompts with illustrations and photos

Award Certificate 241
• certificate to fill in and send home

Handwriting 242
• information on mechanics and grasp patterns
• evaluation checklist
• reproducible practice pages and models

Classroom Behavior Checklist 254
• list of listening and speaking behaviors to post

Who Is That?

Who is that?
It's a very fat cat.
It's a dog with a hat.
Who is that?
It's Sam and Pat!

Phonemic Awareness: short /a/

Name _____

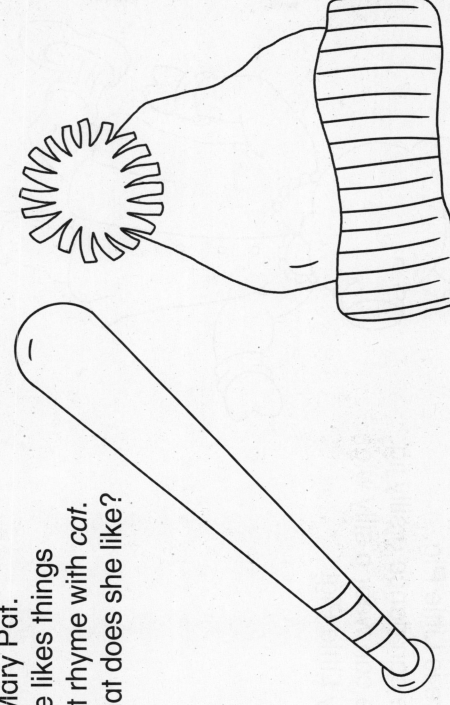

© Macmillan/McGraw-Hill

Mary Pat

My best friend
is Mary Pat.
She likes things
that rhyme with *cat.*
What does she like?

Phonemic Awareness: short /a/

Rhymes and Chimes

Unit 1 • I Can! Can You? (167)

Here Is Little Pig

Here is Little Pig.
She can dance a silly jig.
She can wear a silly wig.
Silly Little Pig!

Phonemic Awareness: short /i/

Name _____

My Pet's Trick

Brad the Crab has just one trick.
And that's okay with me.
When I grab for Brad the Crab,
he runs away from me.

© Macmillan/McGraw-Hill

Phonemic Awareness: blends /br/, /kr/, /gr/, and /tr/

Name _____

Skunk and Chipmunk

Little Skunk went to school.
Chipmunk went there, too.
Chipmunk read his friend a book
about animals in a zoo.
Chip read and read
and then Skunk said,
"I know what we must do.
Let's pretend for the rest of the day
to be jumping kangaroos!"

Phonemic Awareness: blends /nd/, /st/, /nt/, and /nk/

Rhymes and Chimes

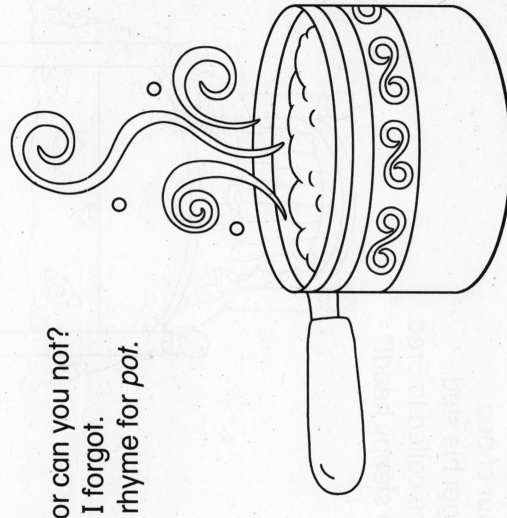

© Macmillan/McGraw-Hill

Hot Pot!

Hot pot! Hot pot!
Can you rhyme, or can you not?
I can rhyme, but I forgot.
Help me make a rhyme for *pot*.

Phonemic Awareness: short /o/

Ned and Fred

Ned got up and out of bed.
Then he went to get his sled.
"The snow fell!" he called to Fred.
"Get up now, you sleepy head!"

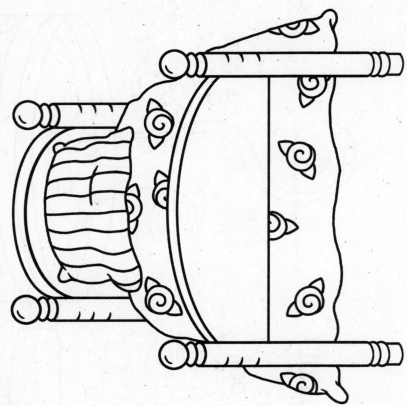

Phonemic Awareness: short /e/

© Macmillan/McGraw-Hill

A Cub Scout's Birthday

Shout, shout,
Shout it out!
Today is the birthday
Of this Cub Scout.
His face has a smile,
Not a pout!

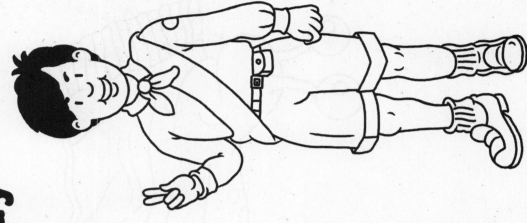

Phonemic Awareness: /sh/ and /th/

A Hug for a Slug

A slug on a rug
wasn't happy or snug.
It took a short run,
had fun in the sun,
And found someone
to give it a hug!

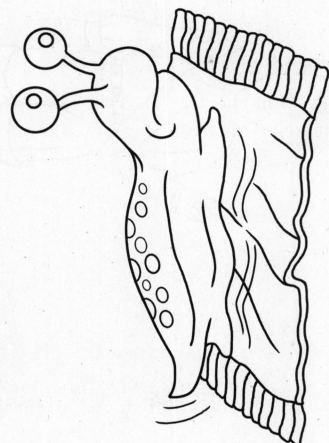

Phonemic Awareness: rhyme and short /u/

Name _____

Play Day

Gingerbread kids went out to play.
The sky was clear and blue.
They flew a kite
slid down a hill,
and were glad the whole day through!

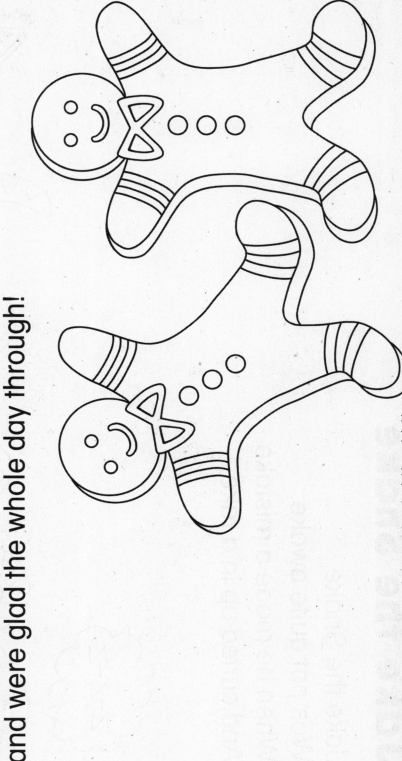

Phonemic Awareness: rhyme, blends /sl/ and /pl/

Name _____

Jake the Snake

Jake the Snake
Was not quite awake,
When he made a mistake
And curled up in a rake.

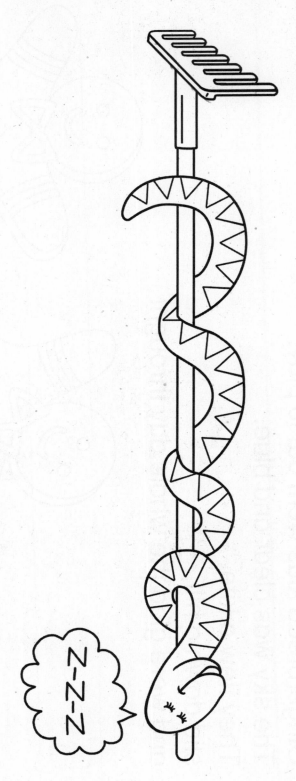

Phonemic Awareness: long /ā/

© Macmillan/McGraw-Hill

Name _____

My Hound Dog

Sniff, sniff, goes the
slow hound, Spot.
He sticks his nose to
the ground.
He smells all the things
his nose comes upon,
and swishes his tail
around.

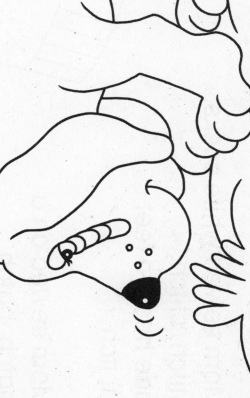

Phonemic Awareness: /sn/ *sn-*

Rhymes and Chimes

Name _____

Mom's Socks

When Mom sewed white socks,
stitch, stitch, stitch,
they made her her two feet
itch, itch, itch.

When Mom sewed on a
patch, patch, patch,
her white socks didn't
match, match, match.

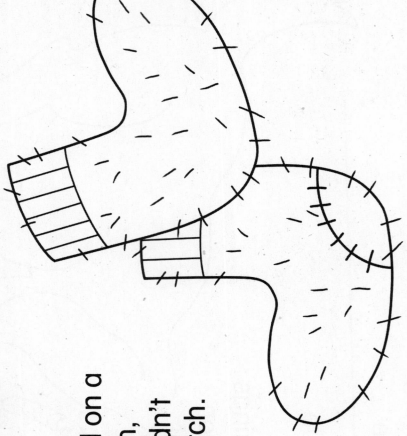

© Macmillan/McGraw-Hill

Phonemic Awareness: rhyme, /ch/, and /hw/

The Missing Dime

Who stole the goose's dime?
When was it taken?
What was the time?
Goodness! Gracious!
What a crime!

Phonemic Awareness: long /ī/

It's Spring

It's Spring! It's Spring!
Let's go to the stream!
Let's splash in the water
and let out a scream!

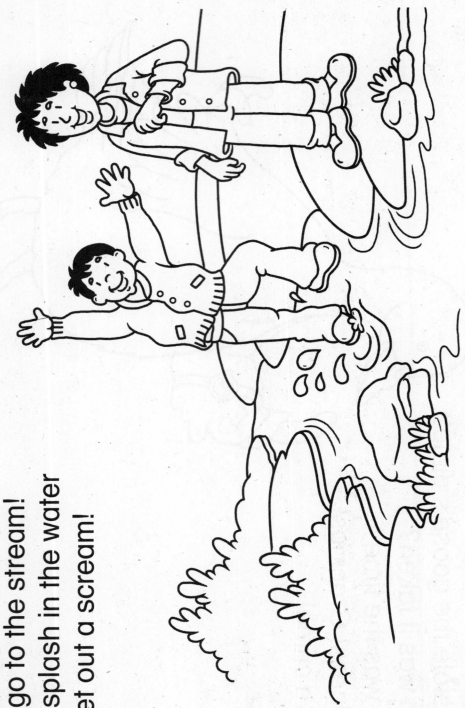

Phonemic Awareness: triple-consonant blends /skr/, /spl/, /spr/, and /str/

Name _____

The Dragon Spoke

With a puff of smoke,
The Dragon spoke.
"Tell me a story!
Tell me a joke!"

Phonemic Awareness: /ō/ o_e

Name _____

A Tune in June

I learned to play the flute
one day in sunny June.
I thought it sounded cute,
my funny, happy tune!

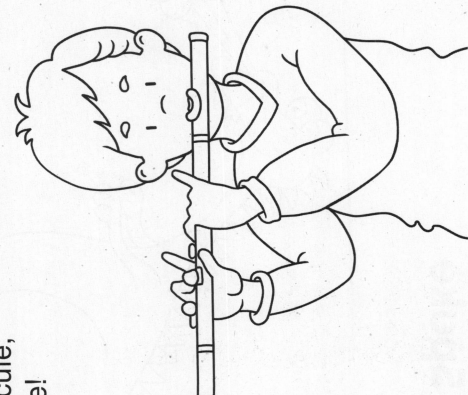

Phonemic Awareness: long /ū/

Fishing Today

Today we're going fishing.
We're going to the lake.
I will take the poles and
Joe will bring the bait.
Yes, today we're going fishing,
And I can hardly wait!

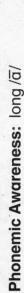

Phonemic Awareness: long /ā/

Sweet Pete

My dog Pete is really sweet.
He loves to say hello.
So if you greet him
on the street
He might not let you go!

Phonemic Awareness: long /ē/

Rhymes and Chimes

Puppy or Guppy?

Would you be happy
If you wanted a puppy
And your mommy or daddy
Got you a guppy?

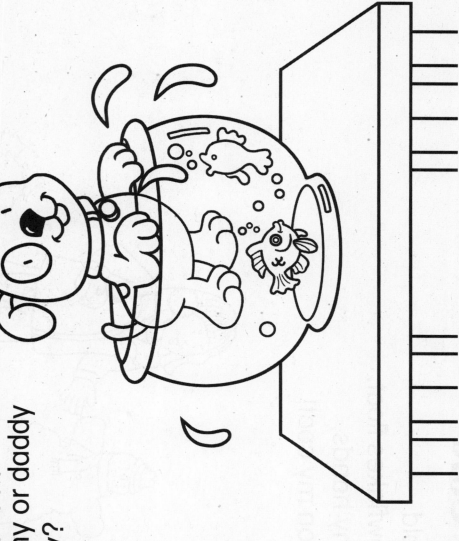

Phonemic Awareness: final long /ē/

Out in the Cold

I go out in the cold
to watch the snowflakes float.
I hold out both my hands,
but they land upon my coat!

Phonemic Awareness: long /ō/

Name _____

Dwight the Knight

Dwight the Knight
Was afraid he might
Meet a wild monster
And have to fight.
Did he try one night?

Phonemic Awareness: long /ī/

If I Saw an Alligator

If I saw an alligator
with teeth so sharp,
I'd say I was busy
and quickly depart!

Phonemic Awareness: r-controlled vowel /är/

Name _____

Chores in the Morn

It's time for chores
at Old North Farm
and the dog howls for food by the door.
The horse gets some hay,
the chickens peck corn,
and the old cow keeps mooing for more.

Phonemic Awareness: /ôr/

Covered with Dirt

Look at my shirt!
Look at your skirt!
We're covered with dirt,
but we didn't get hurt!

Phonemic Awareness: /ûr/

No Rain to be Found

The river is low.
The water is brown.
It hasn't rained.
No drops came down.
Wait!
The clouds are gray.
We shout, "Hooray!"
We'll play in the house
on a rainy day.

Phonemic Awareness: /ou/

© Macmillan/McGraw-Hill

Take a Look

Snuggle up in your own little nook,
or sit beside a bubbling brook.
Be sure to take a special book.
Open it up and take a look!

Phonemic Awareness: /ù/

At the Fair

We went to the fair at noon.
We rode the Loop-the-Loop,
ate ice cream by the scoop,
and each got a big red balloon!

Phonemic Awareness: variant vowel /ü/

Name _____

My Pup Paul

My pup Paul cannot be taught
That toys are to be chased and caught.
After running around, he likes to yawn
And pause for a nap on the shady lawn.

© Macmillan/McGraw-Hill

Phonemic Awareness: variant vowel /ô/

Name _____

Birthday Boy

Point him out,
The birthday boy!
We all brought gifts
We hope he'll enjoy.
Happy birthday,
Edward Roy!

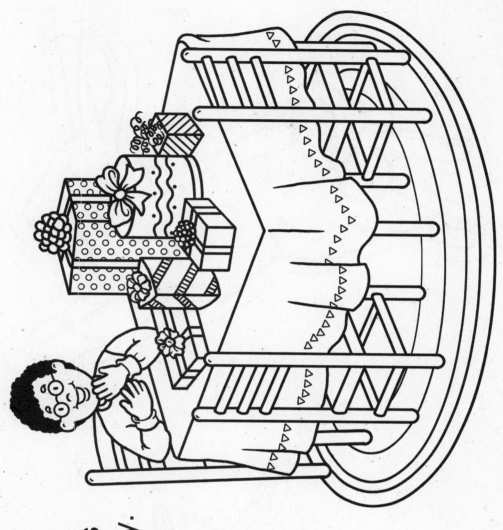

Phonemic Awareness: rhyme and /oi/

Story Patterns

Name _____

Story Patterns

Name _____

Story Patterns

Name _____

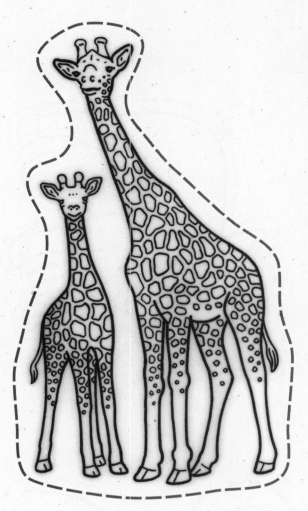

Story Patterns

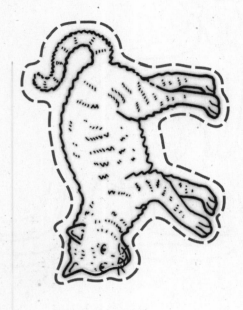

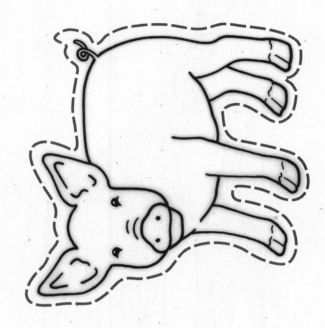

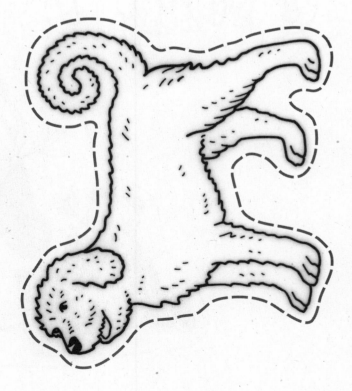

Story Patterns

Name _____

Story Patterns

Name _____

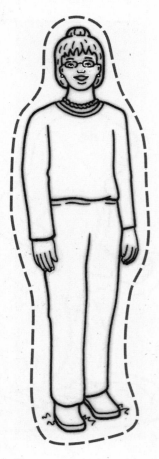

Story Patterns

Name _____

© Macmillan/McGraw-Hill

Story Patterns

Story Patterns

© Macmillan/McGraw-Hill

Name _____

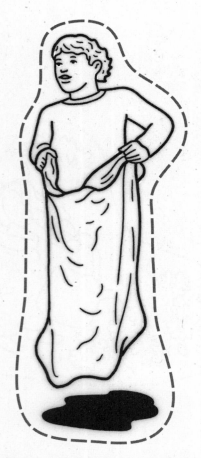

Name _____

Unit 3 • Smile, Mike!

Story Patterns

© Macmillan/McGraw-Hill

Name _____

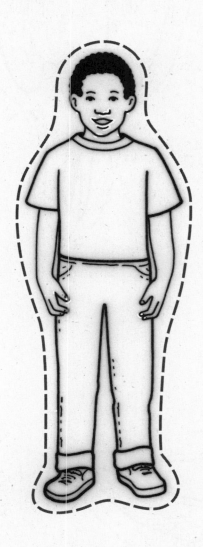
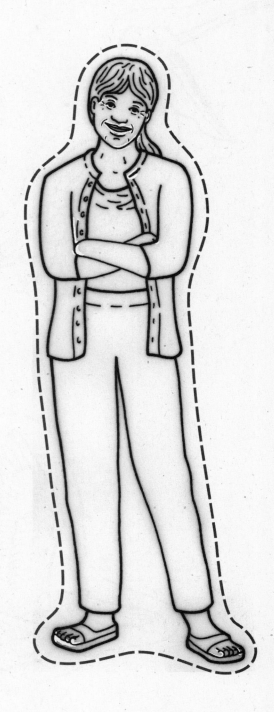

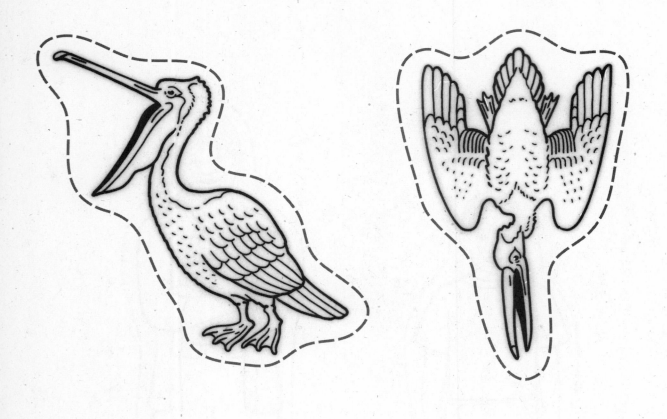

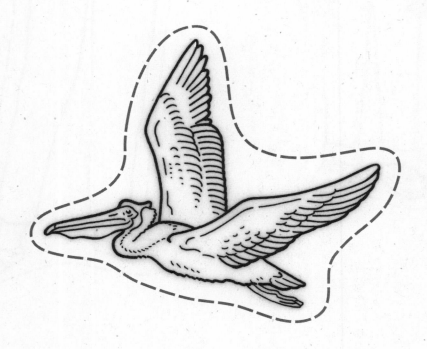

Story Patterns

Name _____

Story Patterns

Unit 4 • June Robot Cleans Up (213)

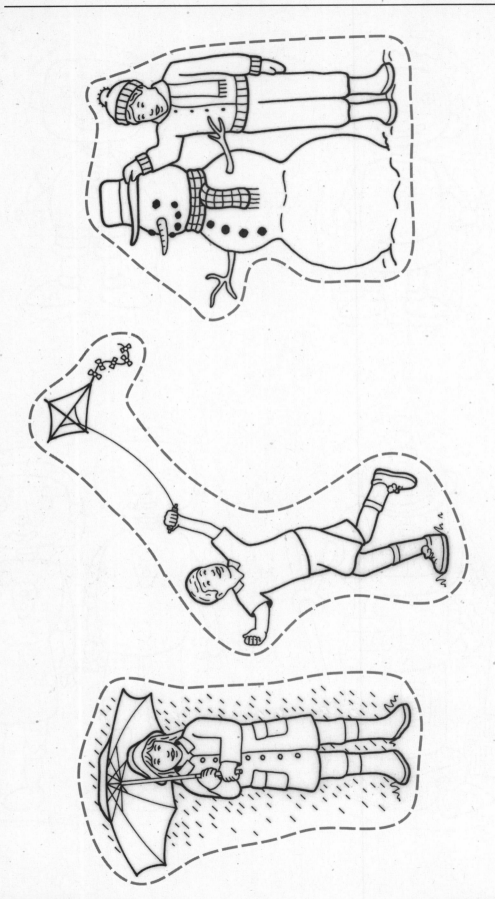

Story Patterns

Name _____

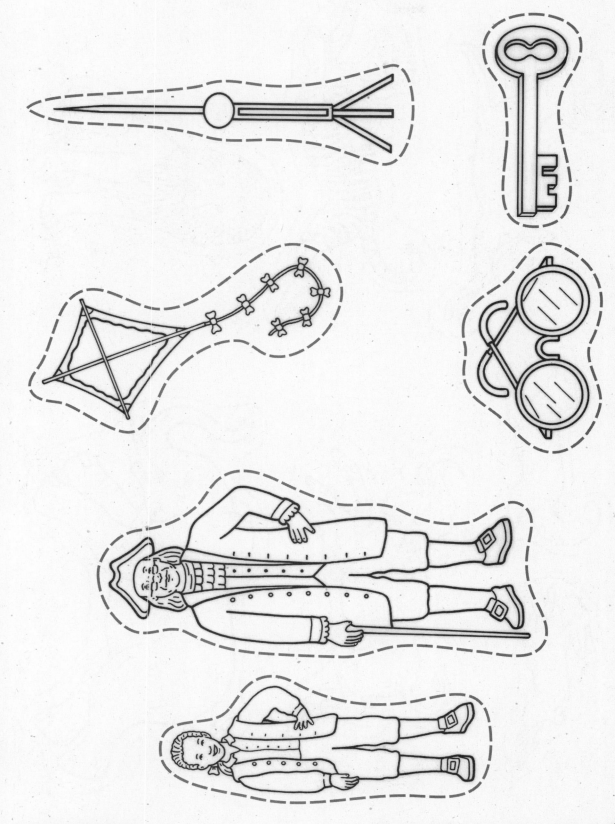

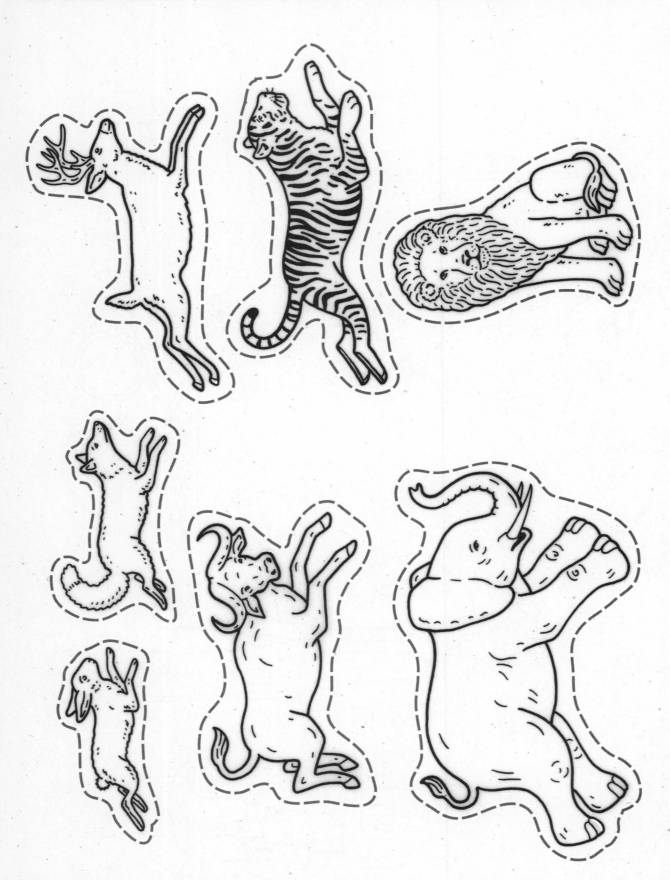

Story Patterns

Name _____

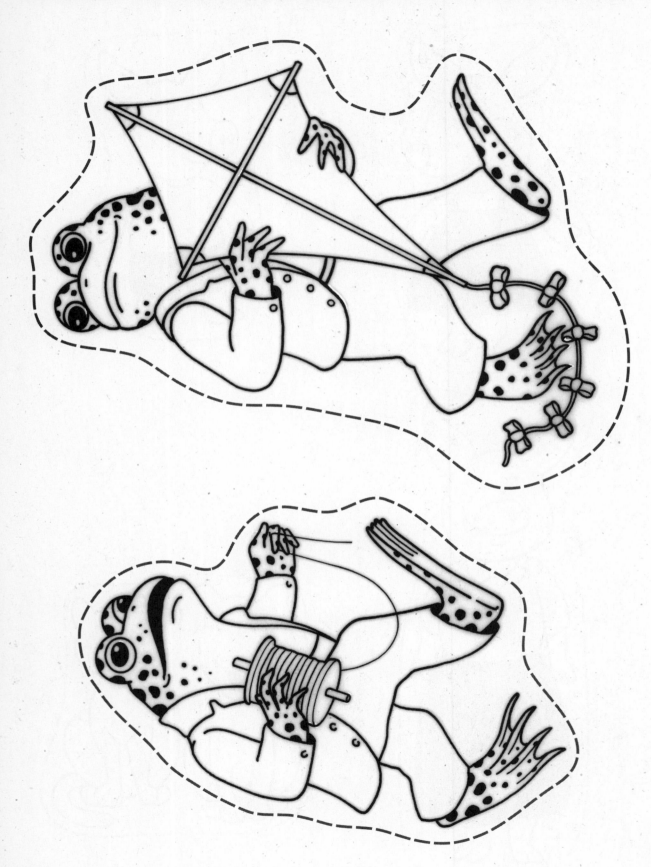

Story Patterns

Name _____

Name _____

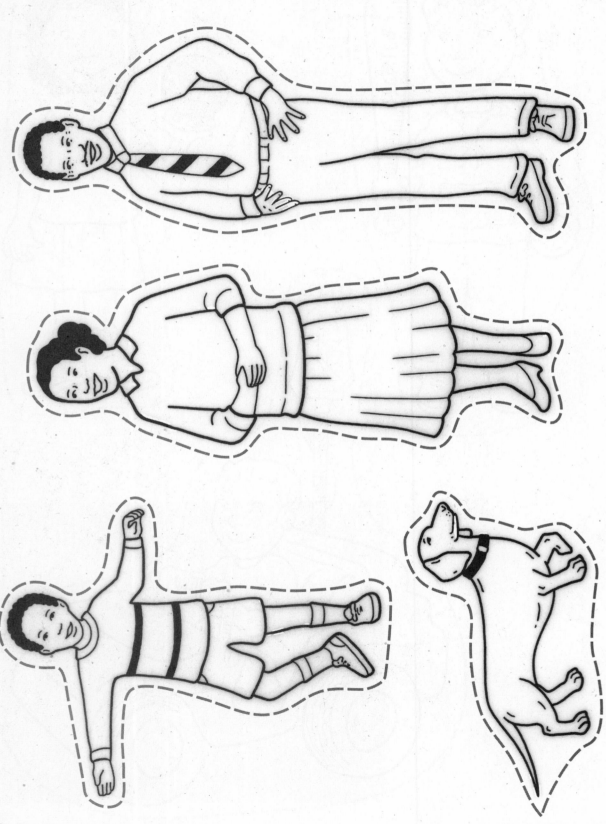

Story Patterns

Name _____

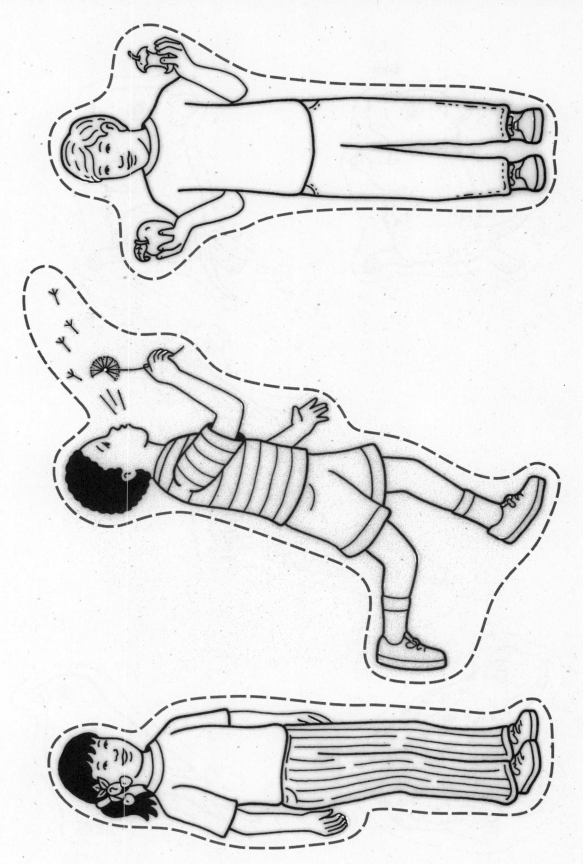

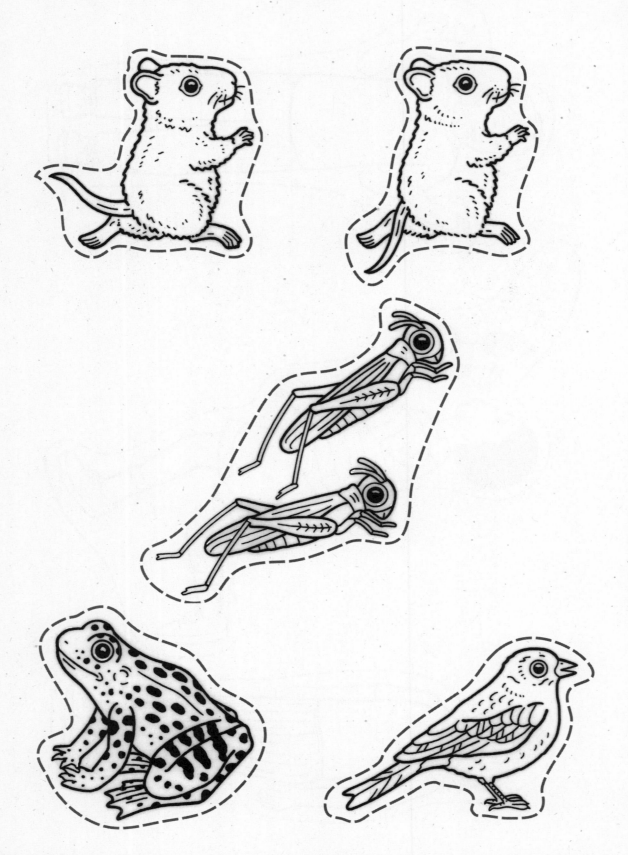

Unit 6 • Dot and Jabber and the Big Bug Mystery   **Story Patterns**

Name _____

Story Patterns

Unit 6 • Little Bear Goes to the Moon (223)

Name _____

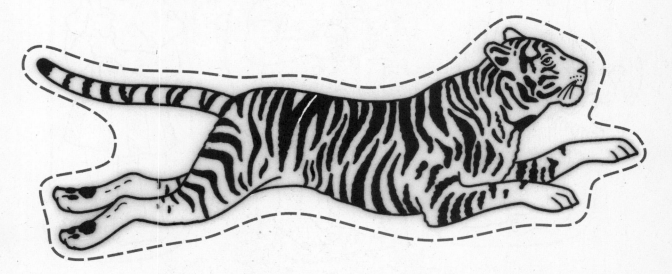

Name _____

Story Patterns

Name _____

Reader Response

Title of Book: _____

Author: _____

How did you like this book? Circle a face.

Liked

Okay

Disliked

Response: Draw a picture of a character from the book. Use the author's description in your drawing.

Name _____

Reader Response

Title of Book: _____

Author: _____

How did you like this book? Circle a face.

Liked   Okay   Disliked

Response: Draw a picture of a scene from the book. Label the parts of the picture.

Reader Response: Nonfiction

Name _____

Reader Response

Title of Book: _____

Author: _____

How did you like this book? Circle a face.

Liked

Okay

Disliked

Response: Choose a word that you liked in the poem. Draw a picture of how you feel that word looks.

Name _____

My Writer's Checklist
Fiction

Read each question. Circle your answer.

Do I have a main character?	☺ Yes	☹ No
Do I tell about interesting events?	☺ Yes	☹ No
Do I use descriptive words?	☺ Yes	☹ No
Do I have a beginning, middle, and end?	☺ Yes	☹ No
Do I begin each sentence with a capital letter?	☺ Yes	☹ No

How did I do?

Draw a face to show how you feel about your work.

Teacher: The main character can be the child in first person. See also Proofreading Marks, page 232, and the Writing Rubric, page 233.

Writer's Checklist

Name _____

My Writer's Checklist
Nonfiction

Read each question. Circle your answer.

Do I have a main idea?	☺ Yes	☹ No
Do I have supporting details?	☺ Yes	☹ No
Do I start with a sentence that tells what my topic is?	☺ Yes	☹ No
Do I explain my topic for my reader?	☺ Yes	☹ No
Do I end each sentence with a punctuation mark?	☺ Yes	☹ No

How did I do?

Draw a face to show how you feel about your work.

Teacher: See also Proofreading Marks, page 232, and the Writing Rubric, page 233.

Proofreading Marks

≡ Make a capital letter.

we went to the park.
≡

∧ Add.

Then ∧ate lunch.
     we

𝓎 Take out.

The tall trees were very tall.

Writing Rubric

	Excellent 4	Good 3	Fair 2	Unsatisfactory 1

Writing to a Picture Prompt

Children are sometimes asked to write about a picture instead of just responding to a writing prompt. The child will either tell about what they see in the picture, or write about something related to the picture. The form of the writing is usually a story or an essay.

Use the picture prompts as additional writing practice or to help children prepare for writing tasks on standardized tests.

Instruct children to do the following:

Before Writing

1. Look closely at the picture. Think about what is happening in the picture.
2. Ask yourself questions about the picture:
   - Where and when are the events shown in the picture taking place?
   - Who or what is in the picture? What are they doing?
   - Can you tell what is happening? What event may have happened prior to this one? What do you think might happen next?
3. You can use a graphic organizer to organize your ideas before you begin to write. You can also make an outline, create an idea web, or do other prewriting work.

During Writing

Use a graphic organizer, or other prewriting work, to write about what is happening in the picture.

After Writing

1. Use the Writer's Checklists, pages 230–231, to help you check your writing.
2. Proofread your writing using Proofreading Marks, page 232.

Write to a picture prompt. Look at the picture. What have you learned to do? Write about it.

_____

_ _ _ _ _ _ _ _ _ _ _ _ _ _ _ _ _ _ _ _

_____

_ _ _ _ _ _ _ _ _ _ _ _ _ _ _ _ _ _ _ _

_____

© Macmillan/McGraw-Hill

Write to a picture prompt. Look at the picture. What animal homes does the diver see? Write about it.

_____

- -

_____

- -

_____

- -

_____

Name _____

Write to a picture prompt. Look at the picture. What do you like to do on a sunny day? Write about it.

_____

_____

_____

_____

_____

Name _____

Write to a picture prompt. Look at the photograph. What would you like to do on a snowy day? Write about it.

Picture Prompts

Name _____

Write to a picture prompt. Look at the picture. What kind of toy would you like to invent? Write about it.

Name _____

Write to a picture prompt. Look at the photograph. What job would you like to do? Write about it.

1

WOW!

NAME _____

MOM!

DATE _____

SIGNED _____

Award Certificate

Handwriting

A Communication Tool

Although computers are available, many tasks require handwriting. Keeping journals, completing forms, taking notes, making shopping or organizational lists, and reading handwriting are practical uses of this skill.

Writing Readiness

Before children begin to write, they need to develop certain fine motor skills. These are examples of warm-up activities:

- Play "Simon Says" using fingers only.
- Sing finger plays such as "Where Is Thumbkin?" and "The Eensie Weensie Spider," or sing songs that use Signed English or American Sign Language.
- Use mazes that require children to move their writing instruments from left to right.

Determining Handedness

Keys to determining handedness in a child:

- With which hand does the child eat? This hand is likely to become the dominant hand.
- Does the child start coloring with one hand and then switch to the other? This may be due to fatigue or lack of hand preference.
- Does the child cross midline to pick things up? Place items directly in front of the child to see if one hand is preferred.
- Does the child do better with one hand or the other?

The Mechanics of Writing

Desk and Chair

- Chair height should allow feet to rest flat on the floor.
- Desk height should be two inches above the level of the elbows when the child is sitting.

- There should be an inch between the child and the desk.
- The child should sit erect with elbows resting on the desk.
- Models of letters should be on the desk or at eye level.

Paper Position

- Right-handed children should turn the paper so that the lower left-hand corner of the paper points to the abdomen.

- Left-handed children should turn the paper so that the lower right-hand corner of the paper points to the abdomen.

- The nondominant hand should anchor the paper near the top so that the paper doesn't slide.
- The child should move the paper up as he or she nears the bottom of the paper. Many children do not think of this.

The Writing Instrument Grasp

The writing instrument must be held in a way that allows for fluid dynamic movement.

Functional Grasp Patterns

- <u>Tripod Grasp</u> The writing instrument is held with the tip of the thumb and the index finger and rests against the side of the third finger. The thumb and index finger form a circle.

Handwriting Basics

- <u>Quadrupod Grasp</u> The writing instrument is held with the tip of the thumb and index finger and rests against the fourth finger. The thumb and index finger form a circle.

Incorrect Grasp Patterns

- <u>Fisted Grasp</u> The writing instrument is held in a fisted hand.

- <u>Pronated Grasp</u> The writing instrument is held diagonally within the hand with the tips of the thumb and index finger on the writing instrument but with no support from other fingers.

- <u>Five-Finger Grasp</u> The writing instrument is held with the tips of all five fingers.

- <u>Flexed or Hooked Wrist</u> A flexed or bent wrist is typical with left-handed writers and is also present in some right-handed writers.

Correcting Grasp Patterns

- Have children play counting games with an eye dropper and water.
- Have children pick up small objects with a tweezer.
- Have children pick up small coins using just the thumb and index finger.
- To correct wrist position, have children check their posture and paper placement.

Evaluation Checklist

Formation and Strokes

☑ Do letters begin at the top?
☑ Do circles close?
☑ Are the horizontal lines straight?
☑ Do circular shapes and extender and descender lines touch?
☑ Are the heights of all capital letters equal?
☑ Are the heights of all lowercase letters equal?
☑ Are the lengths of the extenders and descenders the same for all letters?
☑ Do the letters rest on the line?

Directionality

☑ Are letters and words formed from left to right?
☑ Are letters and words formed from top to bottom?

Spacing

☑ Are the spaces between letters equal?
☑ Are the spaces between words equal?
☑ Are spaces between sentences equal?
☑ Are the top, bottom, and side margins even?

Handwriting Basics

Name _____

Write the letters.

A A A

a a a

B B B

b b b

C C C

c c c

D D D

d d d

Handwriting Practice

Name _____

Write the letters.

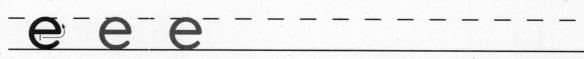

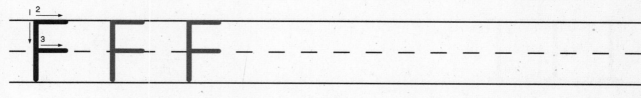

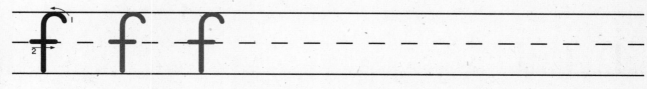

Name _____

Write the letters.

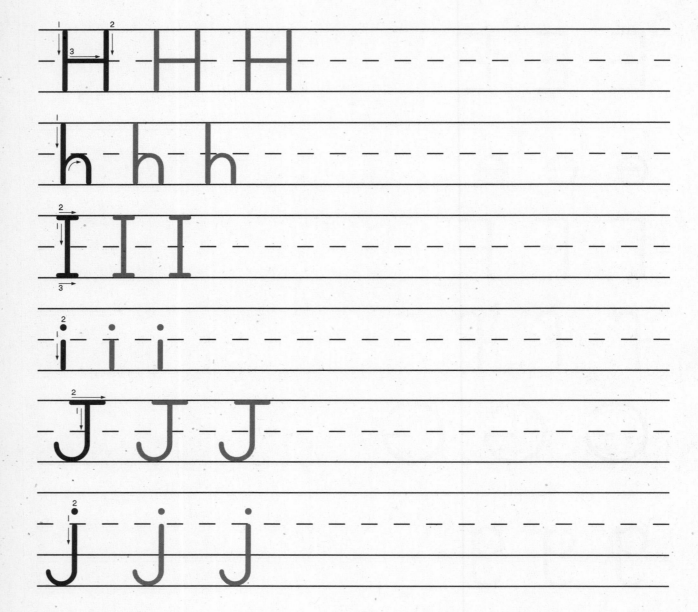

Handwriting Practice

Name _____

● Write the letters.

K K K – – – – – – – – – – – – – –

k k k – – – – – – – – – – – – – –

L L L – – – – – – – – – – – – – –

I I I – – – – – – – – – – – – – –

M M M – – – – – – – – – – – – –

m m m – – – – – – – – – – – – –

N N N – – – – – – – – – – – – –

n n n

© Macmillan/McGraw-Hill

Handwriting Practice (247)

Name _____

Write the letters.

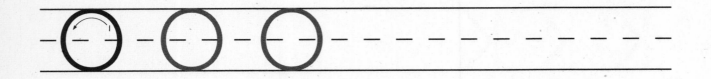

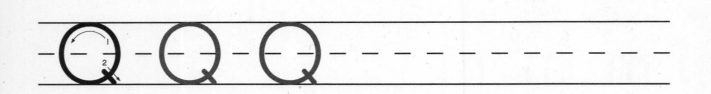

Handwriting Practice

Name _____

Write the letters.

R R R

r r r

S S S

s s s

T T T

t t t

Handwriting Practice

Name _____

Write the letters.

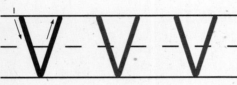

Handwriting Practice

Name _____

- Write the letters.

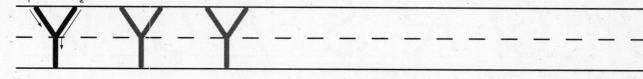

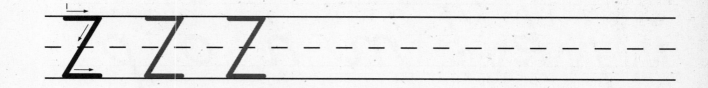

Handwriting Models – Slant

A B C D E F G H
I J K L M N O
P Q R S T U V
W X Y Z

a b c d e f g h
i j k l m n o p
q r s t u v w
x y z

Handwriting Models

Name _____

Handwriting Practice

Good Listening and Speaking Habits

In our classroom we:

- Follow class procedures and rules

- Respect other people's feelings and ideas

- Speak clearly so that others can understand

- Listen to one another thoughtfully

- Take turns speaking

- Do not criticize people because of their ideas

- Ask good questions

- Answer questions thoughtfully

- Do our best and encourage others to do their best

Classroom Behavior Checklist